MY MOTHER'S BETRAYAL

A TALE OF LOVE, REVELATION, AND SURVIVAL

SONIA PULLOCK

Copyright © 2024 **K.F. Publishing**

All rights reserved. No part of this publication may be reproduced, distributed, or transmitted in any form or by any means, including photocopying, recording, or other electronic or mechanical methods, without the prior written permission of the publisher, except in the case of brief quotations embodied in critical reviews and certain other noncommercial uses permitted by copyright law. For permission requests, write to the publisher, addressed "Attention: Book Rights and Permission," at the address below.

Published in the United States of America

ISBN 978-1-963379-63-1 (SC)
ISBN 978-1-963379-62-4 (Ebook)

K.F. Publishing
44 Greene Dr Brampton,
ON L6V 2R7, Canada
brookssonia36@gmail.com

Order Information and Rights Permission:

Quantity sales. Special discounts might be available on quantity purchases by corporations, associations, and others. For details, contact the publisher at the address above.

For Book Rights Adaptation and other Rights Permission. Call us at toll-free 1-888-945-8513 or send us an email at admin@stellarliterary.com.

Dedication Page:

To my beloved granddaughter, KF,

This book is lovingly dedicated to you, my courageous and resilient angel. As you face this formidable battle against severe disease, I am in awe of your immense strength and bravery, much like the main character within these pages.

You have always been an inspiration to me, displaying unwavering determination and an indomitable spirit even in the face of adversity. Just like the protagonist in this book, you have the power to persevere, to overcome any obstacles that lie ahead, and to emerge stronger, wiser, and filled with an abundance of hope and light.

May the pages of this story serve as a gentle reminder that you are never alone in this journey. With every word, every sentence, and every chapter, I hope to transport you to a world brimming with boundless possibilities and endless moments of joy, providing you with a temporary escape from the challenges you face.

Never forget that miracles can happen within the realm of literature, and imagination and dreams can unfold. It is my dearest wish that this book becomes your sanctuary, filling your heart with hope, igniting your imagination, and reminding you that you are capable of accomplishing great things.

Through the highs and lows, the victories and setbacks, always remember that I am by your side, cheering you on with unwavering love and support. You are a beacon of strength, my warrior, and I am eternally proud to call you, my granddaughter.

With all my love,
Grandma Sonia

The characters and the names in this book are fictional and do not represent real individuals. Any resemblance to actual persons or places is purely coincidental. The author has taken great care to ensure the anonymity and privacy of all individuals involved. The events and situations depicted are inspired by real-life experiences but have been altered to protect the identities of those involved. Any similarities to real-life events or individuals should not be interpreted as intentional or reflective of actual events or persons.

Prologue

Marva never imagined that her life would take such a tragic turn. She was just a young girl, filled with dreams and aspirations for her future. But fate had other plans for her, and soon, she found herself entangled in a web of deceit and danger.

At a tender age, Marva found herself facing an unexpected pregnancy. Her mother, Sarah, realized that she needed to find a way to end her relationship with Richard, her former lover. In a shocking and heartbreaking decision, she arranged for Marva to be sold to him.

With promises of a better life for the young girl, Richard became the unsuspecting savior in this treacherous situation. However, behind his charming facade lay a hidden secret that would plague their lives.

As Marva delved into her new life with Richard, she discovered the dark underbelly of her mother's betrayal. Richard, once Sarah's lover, was revealed to be a dangerous and manipulative individual, entwined in a world of crime and violence.

Trapped in a life she never chose, Marva faced unimaginable hardships as Richard asserted control over her. Driven by her determination to protect herself and her child, Marva resolved to escape Richard's clutches. But the threat only intensified with each passing day, and she must confront her deepest fears, trust unlikely allies, and summon unparalleled strength to break free from the treacherous prison that Richard had created.

This is the story of Marva's fight for survival and her quest for truth and redemption. A tale of love, revelation, and survival that will keep readers on the edge of their seats.

Contents

Dedication Page: iii
Prologue v
Chapter 1: A Lonely Childhood 1
Chapter 2: Unforeseen Desires 4
Chapter 3: The Unplanned Arrival 9
Chapter 4: The Heart-Wrenching Decision 14
Chapter 5: The Tangled Web of Love 19
Chapter 6: Trapped in Misery 25
Chapter 7: Alone in Darkness 29
Chapter 8: A Grip on Hope 35
Chapter 9: Shattered Dreams 43
Chapter 10: Escape from the Shadows 54
Chapter 11: Fighting for Freedom 63
Chapter 12: Rebuilding a Life 74
Chapter 13: From Darkness to Hope 83
Chapter 14: Unexpected Ending 88
Authors Biography 94

Chapter 1: A Lonely Childhood

Marva grew up in St. Ann, Jamaica, in a small house on the outskirts of town. Alongside her lived her two older sisters, her mother, Sarah, and her strict grandmother. They resided on her grandmother's property, a place filled with rules and expectations that Marva often struggled to meet.

From an early age, Marva knew that her family was different from the others. Her mother, Sarah, was often absent, leaving Marva to fend for herself. Her father was never in the picture, but Marva knew who he was, and he's already married to another woman. Her mother rarely spoke of him; when she did, it was with bitterness and anger.

Marva's childhood was a lonely one. Despite having her sisters around, their relationship was strained, and they rarely found solace in each other's company. They had their own battles to fight and burdens to bear. Marva had no one to turn to when she needed comfort or support. Her mother often left her with one of her friends during the day and picked her up at night, leaving Marva to wonder why.

Marva never knew why her mother did this. Maybe it was to work, or maybe it was to spend time with her own friends. Whatever the reason, Marva learned to be self-sufficient and take care of herself and her needs. She became adept at cooking simple meals, doing household chores, and finding ways to entertain herself.

She spent her days exploring the fields around her home, finding solace in the beauty of nature. The vibrant colors of the flowers, the soothing sound of the river, and the gentle rustling of the trees became her companions. She would sit by the river and watch the fish swim by or climb trees to get a better view of the world. In these moments, she felt a sense of peace that she couldn't find within the walls of her home.

Marva was a bright child, and despite her difficult upbringing, she excelled in school. Her teachers recognized her potential and encouraged her to pursue her dreams. But Marva knew that her dreams would be hard to achieve without the support of her family. She longed for the love and care other children had, for the warmth and affection of a mother and father.

As she grew older, Marva began to realize that her mother would never be the mother she needed. The emotional distance between them grew, and conversations became scarce. She would have to find her own way in the world, relying on her strength and resilience to overcome the obstacles ahead.

Marva's footsteps echoed along the cobblestone pathway as she made her way towards her home. With each step, her heart grew heavier, burdened by a sense of unease she couldn't shake. Deep down, Marva yearned for someone to rely on—someone who would understand and support her unconditionally. It was time to seek the answers and the connection she desperately needed.

Chapter 2: Unforeseen Desires

Marva's high school years had been a rollercoaster of emotions, filled with both triumphs and tribulations. While she relished the newfound freedom that came with high school, she also harbored a deep-rooted fear of Richard, an individual whose presence instilled a sense of unease within her. Seeking solace from her anxieties, Marva threw herself wholeheartedly into her studies and focused on building meaningful connections with her peers. Within the walls of her school, she found a refuge, a safe haven where she felt protected.

Driven by a genuine love for learning, Marva immersed herself in her schoolwork. Each subject became a lifeline, allowing her to escape the troubles that plagued her mind. As she dedicated herself to her studies, she excelled in her classes, earning high grades that reflected her immense determination and commitment. Marva eagerly joined various clubs and activities alongside her academic pursuits, seeking connection and companionship.

Through her relentless efforts, Marva discovered a group of friends who soon became her chosen family. Among them, Paul stood out as her closest confidant and the person she trusted implicitly. They shared an unbreakable bond, supporting each other through thick and thin. Aware of Marva's fears, Paul always prioritized creating a safe space for her, offering comfort and security when she needed it most.

Marva sat in the corner of the small room, surrounded by the soft whispers of devoted souls seeking enlightenment. It was a humid summer evening, and she had decided to attend the bible study out of sheer curiosity. She needed a way to break free from the suffocating routine of her own thoughts, to find solace in something greater than herself.

As the discussion progressed, Marva found herself captivated by the words being spoken. Each verse seemed to ignite a tiny spark within her, gently nudging her soul towards a path she had never considered before. Lost in her thoughts, she failed to notice Tony, her neighbor, entering the room.

Tony took a seat next to Marva, his presence a surprise. With a mischievous grin, he leaned in and whispered, "I didn't know you were into this. What's up?"

Marva quickly composed herself and replied, "Nah, I just wanted to learn new things and know more about God. What are you doing here?"

Tony chuckled softly. "Nothing much," he confessed. "I just saw you and thought I'd join in. You know, curiosity killed the cat."

Marva raised an eyebrow, her interest piqued. "And what about you, Tony? Do you believe in divine intervention?"

Tony leaned back and stared into the distance, a hint of melancholy in his eyes. "Yeah, you need some divine intervention too," he muttered under his breath.

Marva let out a half-hearted laugh. "You know what? It's boring, to be honest."

Tony's expression softened, and a glimmer of excitement flashed across his face. "Hey, Marva, come with me. Let's go."

Tony and Marva had been neighbors for as long as they could remember. Their houses stood side by side in their tight-knit community, and they often found themselves walking home together after school.

On this particular evening, as they strolled down the familiar path, their laughter filled the air. The sound of their joy echoed through the quiet streets, capturing the attention of anyone within earshot. Little did they know that a twist of fate awaited them just around the corner.

As Marva giggled at Tony's silly joke, he couldn't help but feel an unfamiliar sensation deep within his chest. His heart skipped a beat, then another, as he realized he was falling in love with Marva. The realization hit him like a ton of bricks, leaving him breathless and uncertain of what to do next.

Their conversation continued, seemingly oblivious to the sudden shift in Tony's emotions. They reached the point where their paths diverged, their houses just a stone's throw away. Taking a leap of faith, Tony mustered up the courage to invite Marva into his empty home.

"Hey, Marva," he said, his voice trembling slightly. "Why don't you come to my house? My parents aren't home, and we can play scrabble and have some snacks." His heart pounded in his chest as he awaited her response.

Marva hesitated for a moment, her eyes scanning the surroundings, but deep down, she knew that no one was expecting her home just yet. "Yeah, I guess I have time for scrabble," she finally agreed, a smile playing on her lips. Little did she know that accepting Tony's invitation would lead her into an unexpected trap.

As they entered Tony's house, the atmosphere seemed to change. The once warm and inviting space now felt cold and eerie. Tony's smile, once filled with genuine innocence, now held a sinister glimmer in his eyes. Marva's instincts screamed at her, warning her of the danger she had unknowingly walked into.

In a dimly lit room, Tony and Marva found themselves alone at home. Tony's intentions were far from honorable, as he plotted to take advantage of Marva. He began to approach her with a sinister glint in his eyes and asked if they could engage in a sexual encounter. Marva's initial response was an immediate and firm "no." She knew in her heart that she did not want this and that she deserved better.

But Tony was relentless. He continued to press her, refusing to accept her rejection. He promised to take precautions to prevent any unwanted consequences, such as pregnancy. Marva's hesitation grew as she felt the weight of Tony's aggression and manipulation bearing down on her. The fear of what he might do if she didn't comply flooded her mind. She couldn't help but wonder, "What if he becomes violent? What if saying 'no' isn't an option?"

Caught between the looming threat of harm and the desire to escape the situation, Marva agrees. Tears streamed down her face as she tried to suppress her emotions, silently enduring the violation she was about to face. It was a moment of utter powerlessness; her body became a mere vessel for Tony's desires.

As soon as the encounter ended, Marva's survival instincts kicked in. She swiftly gathered her clothes, her heart pounding in her chest, and ran away from the scene.

Chapter 3:
The Unplanned Arrival

As the months passed by, Marva couldn't shake off the strange symptoms that plagued her every morning. Nausea, dizziness, and an insatiable hunger seemed to consume her every waking moment. Fear gripped her heart as she considered the possibility that her body was undergoing something unexpected. She couldn't ignore the thought any longer; she made her way to the nearest pharmacy and purchased a pregnancy test.

The minutes ticked by agonizingly slowly as Marva anxiously awaited the test results. Her mind raced with a whirlwind of emotions—fear, confusion, and a glimmer of hope amidst the chaos. Finally, the test revealed what she had feared and secretly hoped for: she was pregnant.

Marva stood frozen, staring at the positive result in her hand. Mixed emotions flooded her being. She felt a swirl of joy, terror, and uncertainty. How could this be happening? How would she face this new chapter in her life, especially after her traumatic experience?

She remembers who the father of the child was; she never told Paul about this, and the thought of facing her mother with the news filled her with dread. Her mother, Sarah, was a stern woman, never one to show affection or compassion. Marva knew that her mother would not take kindly to her news.

Marva kept her secret from her mom, afraid of disclosing that the father was just a neighbor. She knew that she needed to make some difficult decisions. She contemplated her options and thought about what would be best for herself and her unborn child. Though the circumstances were less than ideal, she couldn't help but feel a sense of determination and strength deep within her.

"I can't keep running from the truth. I need to face Tony and tell him the truth about our baby". Marva took a deep breath, wiped away her tears, and decided to gather her courage. The next day, she mustered up enough strength to face him. She knew she needed to talk to Tony and come clean about everything. It was scary, but she had reached a point where she couldn't take it anymore.

As she was walking down the street, Marva spotted Tony talking to his father. She approached them slowly, her heart pounding in her chest. Tony turned around, smiling and waving at her.

"Marva, how's your day?" Tony asked, his voice filled with happiness. Marva got struck; she couldn't move her whole body as she watched him walking slowly towards her. She is struggling; she couldn't bring herself to tell Tony that the baby inside her was his.

Overwhelmed, she ran off in tears, leaving Tony shocked and trying to chase after her to find out what was wrong. However, he was unable to catch her. She got home and locked herself in her room, crying and feeling lost, unsure of what to do next.

The decision to keep her pregnancy a secret from Tony weighed heavily on her. She knew she needed to confront him about the truth, but fear and uncertainty prevented her from doing so earlier.

The next day, her grandmother slowly noticed Marva's secret; she could see bits of vomit in the sink every morning, and Marva's appetite became huge, which led her to suspect that Marva was pregnant. She was furious with Marva and demanded to know what she was thinking. She couldn't believe that this had happened to her granddaughter at the young age of 15. Marva's grandmother immediately called her daughter, Sarah, and relayed the news.

Sarah rushed home after hearing the news relayed by her mother. She didn't believe it at first because Marva is not socially active with other people, but after her mom saw the evidence that she was pregnant, she hung up and went there fast.

She asked her directly, are you pregnant, Marva? Filled with anger and concern. Marva froze, her eyes widening at her mother's abrupt question. The room fell silent, the tension growing thicker by the second. It was a question Marva had hoped to avoid for as long as possible, knowing the reaction it would likely elicit from her mother.

Marva's heartbeat quickened as she weighed her options. She could try to deny it, maybe buy herself some time to gather her thoughts and decide how to approach the situation. However, the truth had an uncanny ability to make its presence known, even in the face of the most desperate attempts to conceal it.

Fighting back the tears, Marva looked into her mother's eyes. "Yes, Mother," she finally admitted softly, her voice trembling. "I am pregnant."

Sarah's face contorted into a mix of disbelief, disappointment, and fury. She struggled to find her voice in the midst of the storm of emotions raging within her. The thought of her daughter, still so young and full of dreams, facing the challenges of motherhood at such an early stage in life weighed heavily on her heart.

Anger surged through Sarah's veins; she was furious and demanded answers. "Who did this to you, Marva? Was it Paul?" Marva hesitated, not wanting her family to discover the truth about what had happened. Fearfully, she nodded and whispered, "Yes, it's Paul's," just to get her mother off her back.

Letting out a heavy sigh, Sarah sat down slowly, her anger fading into a calmer expression like it seemed she had already thought of a plan for her daughter. "Marva, now that the truth is out, I need to figure out what's best for you and the baby," she said, her voice laced with confidence.

As the months went by, Marva delivered a healthy baby boy with her mother, Sarah, by her side. In the midst of the joy and chaos of the delivery room, Sarah couldn't help but feel a sense of unease. She knew that Paul, Marva's supposed boyfriend and the father of the baby, was clueless about the situation.

After the initial excitement settled, Sarah decided it was time to have a difficult conversation with Marva. She gently asked, "Marva, does Paul know about the baby?" Marva shook her head, tears welling up in her eyes. "Yes, he knows," she whispered.

Sarah sighed, conflicted by the weight of the situation. She knew she had to protect her daughter but couldn't ignore the truth. She had made a decision before Marva's birth to take control of the situation. Sarah firmly believed it was in Marva's best interest to have a stable and responsible father figure in her child's life.

So, she registered the child's father as her boyfriend, Richard. Marva was still too young to fully comprehend the weight of the situation; she didn't know what her mother was doing. After she found out that her mother was the one who named the baby, she assumed her mother had her best interests at heart. Marva imagined that her mother and Richard would raise the baby as their own, as her mom had always wanted a boy.

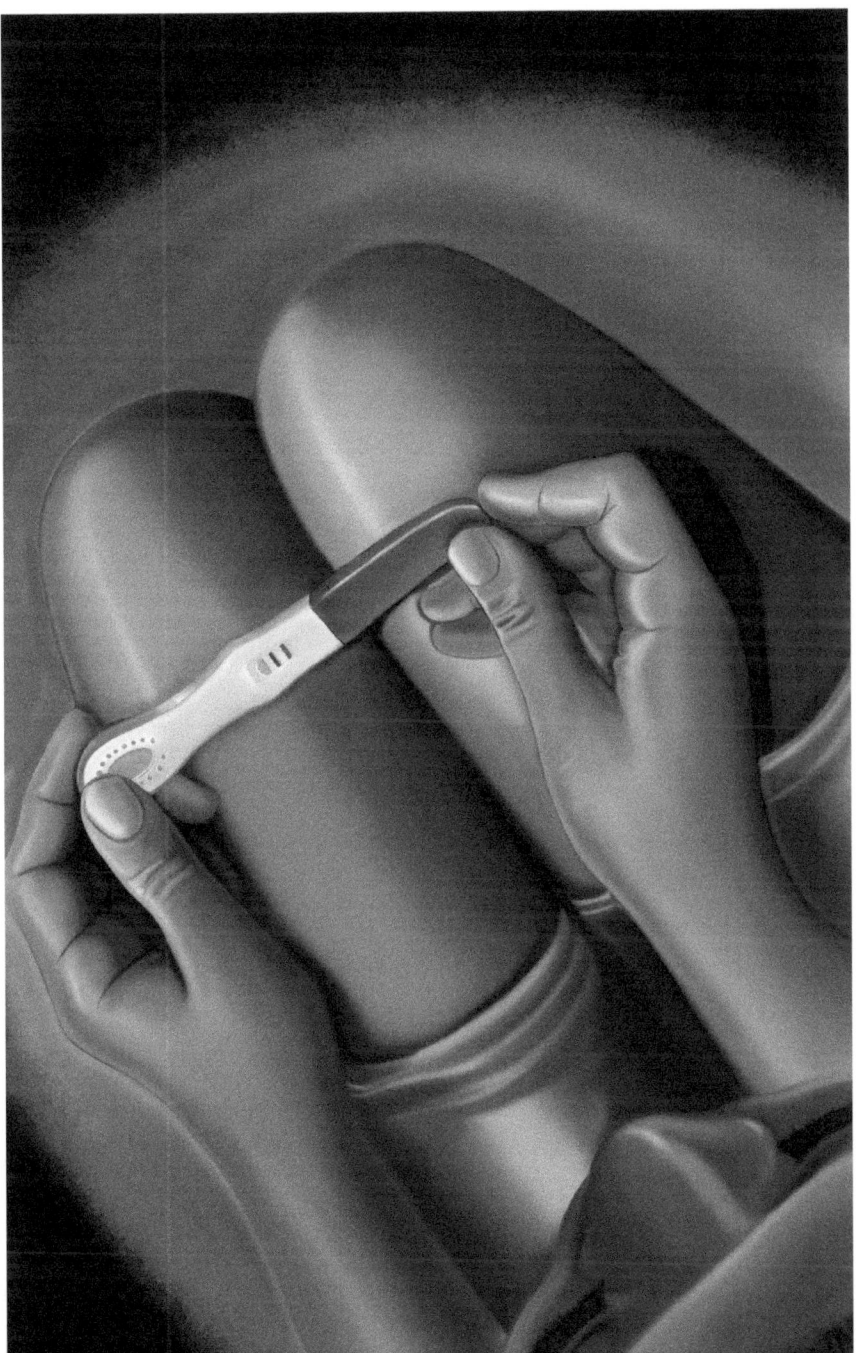

Chapter 4:
The Heart-Wrenching Decision

As Marva settled into the idea that her mother would be taking care of her baby, a sense of relief washed over her. She was just a young girl, barely old enough to understand the complexities of motherhood. Her innocent mind believed that her mother's love would be enough to guide her through this uncertain journey. Little did Marva know that her mother had a sinister plan brewing beneath her seemingly loving facade.

Concealed to Marva, her mother, Sarah, had become entangled in a web of deceit and infidelity. She had been having an affair with a mysterious man whose love had consumed her heart and clouded her judgment. Desperate to escape her relationship with Richard, she saw Marva as a means to an end.

Sarah had always been a master manipulator and saw an opportunity to use Marva as a pawn in her elaborate scheme. With Richard being the financial backbone behind the house they shared on her mother's property, she knew she couldn't simply leave him without consequences. Selling Marva to Richard seemed like the perfect solution, a way to sever ties with Richard while receiving some compensation.

Marva, and her grandmother remained blissfully unaware of Sarah's dark intentions. They continued their lives, oblivious to the betrayal that loomed on the horizon. As Sarah's love for her secret paramour grew stronger, so did her desire to be free from the shackles of her relationship with Richard.

In the midst of the chaos, Marva's grandmother made a drastic decision. After seeing the name of the child's father, she imagined that Richard, who is her mom's boyfriend, had an affair with her granddaughter. She felt disgusted and disappointed for her, so she declared that Marva was no longer welcome in their home. She believed that Marva should face the consequences of her actions and take responsibility for her pregnancy elsewhere.

As Marva's grandmother confronted her about the situation, her voice quivered with anger and disappointment. "I can't believe you've let this happen, Marva," she exclaimed, her eyes filled with tears. "How could you let Richard take advantage of you like this?"

Feeling the weight of her grandmother's words, Marva pleaded, "Grandma, please understand. I didn't plan for any of this to happen. I never wanted to get pregnant; you just don't understand."

Her grandmother's face hardened, and she shook her head in disbelief. "Understand? Do you think this is just some mistake that can be swept under the rug? You've brought shame upon this family, Marva. We can't have you living here anymore. You need to leave."

Marva's heart sank as she realized her grandmother's decision was final. "But Grandma, where will I go? I have nowhere else to turn."

Her grandmother's voice softened slightly, but her resolve remained firm. "That's not my concern, Marva. You need to figure this out on your own. Perhaps it's time for you to grow up and face the reality of your choices."

Marva's grandmother was livid. She couldn't bear the thought of Marva continuing to live under her roof. The situation seemed dire, and they both felt overwhelmed by the weight of it all. Marva's heart sank as she heard her grandmother's words. She felt abandoned and scared, unsure of what her future would hold.

The fateful day finally arrived when Sarah approached Richard with her twisted proposal. She presented Marva to him, her innocent daughter, as if she were nothing more than an object to be sold. Richard, shocked and bewildered, couldn't comprehend the depths of Sarah's betrayal, but because of his lust and having a young girl as one of his sexual desires, he accepted the offer. Sarah smiled, as she was already living a double life, so she was really desperate to be separated from Richard.

Sarah and Richard embarked on the task of finding a new home. As they explored potential houses, they couldn't help but consider the future living arrangements for Marva. Their search for a new home had finally come to an end. They stood together in front of a charming cottage with a white picket fence, envisioning the life they would build within its walls; it's still in St. Ann but farther from their grandma's property.

Marva didn't know; her mother had already made arrangements and found a place to live. She was taken by surprise when her mother abruptly packed their belongings and whisked them away to this new house. As they arrived, the weight of the situation began to sink in. Sarah led Marva to the backyard and set their bags down, her voice trembling as she uttered the words, "I'll go now."

Marva, with confusion and tears streaming down her face, couldn't comprehend what was happening. "Who will live with me here?" she questioned, desperately seeking reassurance and stability in this unexpected turn of events. It was then that Sarah delivered the devastating blow, her voice strained with emotion: "You will be living with this man from now on."

Marva's heart sank as the reality of the situation hit her like a tidal wave. The tears continued to fall, mirroring the shattered dreams and shattered trust she experienced in that very moment. The stable, loving family she had once known was disintegrating before her eyes, leaving her to navigate a new and uncertain path. "Don't cry; I will look for you someday, Sarah added. Marva cried and ran away to her room, hugging her son, confused and unsure of what to do, while her mom just left without saying anything.

Chapter 5:
The Tangled Web of Love

As Sarah's story unfolded, it became clear that her life had been far from simple. Born into a family with four brothers, she was the only girl in the household. Growing up, Sarah's parents had high expectations for her, hoping she would marry well and bring honor to their name. But Sarah had always been headstrong and independent, with dreams of a life beyond the boundaries set by her family.

Working as a vendor in Ocho Rios, a bustling town 12 kilometers away from St. Ann's Bay, Sarah found solace in the chaotic streets and the opportunity to make her own way in the world. She rented a small apartment near her workplace, and every weekend, she would return to her family's home and spend time with her daughter, Marva.

On one of these weekends, Sarah's life took an unexpected turn. As she set up her makeshift stall, selling her wares to the tourists passing by, she noticed a man nearby. He was selling ice cream, his eyes filled with a mysterious allure that drew her in. Intrigued, Sarah struck up a conversation with him, their words mingling with the sounds of the bustling market.

The man's name was Gabriel, and he was a wanderer, much like Sarah herself. He had traveled from afar, seeking adventure and new experiences. As they spent more time together, Sarah found herself captivated by Gabriel's tales of far-off lands and his zest for life. She saw a kindred spirit in him, someone who understood her longing for freedom and independence.

Their connection grew stronger with each passing day, and Sarah found herself falling deeply in love with Gabriel. But their relationship was far from easy. Gabriel had his own demons to wrestle with, and he was also married, making it difficult for them to find a stable foundation for their love to flourish.

Sarah and Gabriel clung to each other despite their challenges, finding solace in their shared dreams and desires. They yearned for a life together, free from the constraints of their pasts. But as the days turned into months, doubts began to creep into Sarah's mind.

Sarah sat alone in her apartment; her mind filled with the complexities of her own past. She had been married once before to a man who had failed to fulfill her emotional needs. Their relationship had grown stagnant, and Sarah had found herself yearning for something more.

Gabriel is married, and Sarah understands. It's common for her in these situations because she easily falls in love with someone. They both agreed on their secret relationship. Since Gabriel and his wife couldn't have children, his dream was to have a baby. Sarah thought about her daughter, whom she had difficulty caring for because of her job. She proposed to Gabriel; you can adopt my daughter. Isn't that what you want? Gabriel is hesitant, but he thinks that his wife will be happy. Sarah believed this arrangement would benefit them both, as it would keep Gabriel's wife occupied and give Sarah more time to focus on her relationship with Gabriel.

"Sarah, I've thought long and hard about your proposal," Gabriel said, his voice filled with both determination and nervousness. "I believe adopting your daughter is the answer we've been searching for. It won't be easy, but I know it's what Maria needs.

She knew her relationship with her boyfriend, Richard, had reached a breaking point. Their love had faded, replaced by resentment and bitterness. Sarah yearned for a fresh start, a chance to build a life with Gabriel, but the complexities of her situation seemed insurmountable.

Sarah and Gabriel continued their journey together; they couldn't help but be consumed by the excitement of their newfound love. They embraced the uncertainty of the future, knowing their bond would be tested in ways they couldn't yet fathom.

As the sun set over Ocho Rios, casting a golden glow over the town, Sarah and Gabriel found comfort in each other's arms. They vowed to face whatever challenges lay ahead, their love acting as a beacon of hope in the darkest times. But little did they know that the storm brewing within their family would soon come crashing down, threatening to shatter their dreams and expose the truth hidden beneath the surface.

On that fateful summer day, Sarah made the decision to take Marva away from her home and bring her to Gabriel's residence in the mountains of St. Ann. Marva's innocent curiosity filled the air as they embarked on their journey. "Where are we going, Mom?" she asked, excitement tinged with a hint of apprehension.

Sarah glanced at Marva, her heart heavy with the weight of the secret she carried. "You'll be staying at my friend's house this summer since I can't come home every weekend," she explained, her voice trembling ever so slightly. "They will take care of you." In her desperation to secure a future with Gabriel, Sarah masked her true intentions with a web of lies, hoping that Marva's innocent trust would shield her from the truth.

As they arrived at their destination, Gabriel was already waiting, his eyes filled with both anticipation and guilt. Marva looked up at Gabriel, her eyes sparkling with hope. "You'll be here for the rest of the summer," Gabriel said, his voice filled with false reassurance, "and then we'll see what happens next."

With those words hanging in the air, Marva watched as her mother left, disappearing into the distance. As they walked towards the house, alone with Gabriel and his wife, Maria, Marva began to sense that things were not as they seemed. Maria's disapproving gaze lingered on her as she didn't expect this; she thought that they were going to adopt an infant, not a girl who was approaching teenage, and Marva couldn't help but feel like an unwanted intruder in their home.

Days turned into weeks, and Marva's discomfort grew. She longed for her mother's presence, for the familiar warmth of her embrace. With each passing day, the truth began to unravel before her eyes. Gabriel's true colors were revealed, and Marva became a victim of his and Maria's cruelty. Forced to shoulder the burden of the household chores, Marva found herself trapped in a never-ending cycle of abuse, both physical and emotional.

As the summer came to an end, Marva's hopes of returning home were crushed. Gabriel and Maria had no intention of enrolling her in the nearby school. Marva's heart sank, her tears flowing freely. She couldn't understand why her mother had abandoned her or why she had been sold like a commodity.

One day, unable to bear the pain any longer, Marva mustered the courage to confront Gabriel and Maria. Tears streamed down her face as she begged to go home, her voice filled with desperation. Gabriel's conscience couldn't ignore Marva's pleas, and even Maria, burdened by guilt, yearned for Marva to escape their clutches.

Reluctantly, Gabriel agreed to take Marva home. Sarah was furious at her daughter's betrayal, her anger overshadowing any semblance of concern or remorse. She couldn't comprehend why Marva would want to leave the life she had supposedly provided for her.

Marva was twelve years old then, and her innocent trust had been shattered. She now understood the darkness that lay within her mother's heart and the depths she was willing to sink to achieve her own desires. This was the beginning of Marva's journey, a journey filled with pain, betrayal, and a desperate search for the truth.

As Marva left Gabriel's residence, heart heavy with the weight of the experiences, she vowed to uncover the secrets that had torn her family apart. With determination in her eyes, she embarked on a quest for justice, determined to expose the truth and find a way to heal the wounds that had scarred her soul.

Little did Marva know that her journey would lead her down a path filled with unexpected twists and turns. As she delved deeper into her family's dark secrets, she would uncover even more sinister revelations, threatening to upend everything she thought she knew.

It was during this time of turmoil that Sarah's sinister plan took shape. Desperate to sever ties with Richard and secure a future with Gabriel, she saw Marva as a means to an end. In her twisted logic, selling her own daughter seemed like the perfect solution, a way to escape the clutches of her past while receiving some form of compensation.

As Sarah's relationship with Richard deteriorated, her desperation grew. She knew she had to act quickly before her plan unraveled or her guilt consumed her. And so, she approached Richard with her twisted proposal, presenting Marva as nothing more than a pawn in her elaborate scheme.

Chapter 6:
Trapped in Misery

Marva's dreams of finding a stable and loving home had shattered. The initial weeks of living with Richard were fine, but as time went on, his true nature began to reveal itself. What started as innocent requests for household chores soon turned into a nightmare of manipulation, abuse, and control.

Every day, Richard would give Marva a long list of tasks to complete, expecting her to tirelessly clean the house, wash his clothes, and tend to his every need. The pressure to meet his demands became overwhelming, and Marva felt like a prisoner in her own home.

To make matters worse, Richard used his position of power to exploit Marva both emotionally and physically. Every night, he would force himself upon her, using her vulnerability as a weapon to satisfy his own desires. The physical abuse that followed any resistance or disobedience left Marva bruised and broken.

Marva sat on the edge of the bed, her body aching from the bruises. Richard walked into the room, a sinister smile on his face. "Did you finish all the tasks I gave you, Marva?" he sneered.

Marva mustered up the courage to meet his gaze. "Yes, Richard. I did everything you asked," she replied, her voice trembling.

Richard's eyes narrowed, and he grabbed her arm forcefully. "You better not be lying to me," he growled. "You know what happens when you lie."

Tears welled up in Marva's eyes as she winced in pain. "Please, Richard, I can't take this anymore. I'm tired, scared, and just want to be free," she pleaded.

Richard's grip tightened, and he leaned in close. "You think anyone will help you, Marva? You're worthless. No one cares about you," he spat.

Marva's pleas for help fell on deaf ears as Richard isolated her from the outside world. He kept a tight grip on the finances, giving her only a fraction of what she needed to survive. His control over her extended to every aspect of her life, leaving her feeling trapped and hopeless.

Each night, as Marva cried herself to sleep, she clung to the tiny flicker of hope that remained within her. She knew she needed to find a way out of this misery, but the path to freedom seemed impossible to navigate.

In the quiet moments, when Richard's presence loomed large, Marva would whisper words of love and encouragement to her baby. She promised her child a safe, happy, and free future. She knew that her baby deserved a life far removed from the pain they were currently experiencing.

In the depths of her despair, Marva began to formulate a plan. She started secretly saving whatever money she could, stashing away small amounts that she hoped would eventually help her escape. She researched local support organizations, seeking guidance and resources that could provide her with the assistance she desperately needed.

As Marva endured each day, she held onto the belief that her baby was her source of strength. The love she felt for her child propelled her forward, even in the face of seemingly insurmountable obstacles. She knew that she had to be strong not only for herself but also for her baby.

As Marva continued to endure Richard's torment, she remained hopeful that her opportunity for escape would come. She vowed to herself that she would not let him destroy her spirit and determinedly held onto the belief that she was worthy of a better life.

Though she felt powerless and believed no one would aid her, Marva's love for her baby fueled her resilience. She knew that she had to endure the suffering for the sake of her child, and she clung to the hope that one day, they would find a way out of this misery.

In the depths of her despair, Marva found solace in her prayers. She would close her eyes, whispering softly in the darkness, hoping that a higher power would hear her cries and provide her with the strength to endure. She held onto the belief that there must be a purpose to her pain and that one day, a door would open, leading her to a life free from Richard's abuse.

Days turned into weeks, weeks turned into months, and Marva's situation remained unchanged. She continued to endure Richard's torment, feeling powerless and alone. The thought of escaping seemed like an impossible dream, but she refused to let go of the hope that flickered within her.

Little did Richard know that Marva's strength was building, and the moment of her liberation was drawing near. She had endured enough pain and suffering, and her determination to break free was unyielding.

She held onto the hope that one day, somehow, they would find a way to escape the clutches of Richard's abuse. Marva's love for her baby became her guiding light in the depths of her misery, reminding her that she was not alone and had the strength to endure for a brighter future.

Chapter 7:
Alone in Darkness

Marva's world had become a relentless nightmare. Richard's abusive behavior continued to escalate, leaving her broken and trapped in a life she never anticipated. The weight of her responsibilities as a young mother to their son burdened her, while Richard treated her like a servant, never showing an ounce of compassion.

Marva sat alone in the dimly lit kitchen, exhausted from the day's struggles. As she nursed her infant son, her mind replayed the events that had led her to this dark place.

"Why does he treat me this way?" she wondered aloud, tears streaming down her face. "All I've ever wanted was to get out of this prison."

Just then, Richard burst through the door, reeking of alcohol. "Where's my dinner, woman?" he slurred angrily.

Marva flinched at his booming voice. "I-I'm sorry, it's not ready yet. The baby needed me," she replied meekly.

Richard stormed over, grabbing her arm roughly. "I don't care about your excuses! You're useless," he spat.

Marva felt the weight of Richard's expectations crushing her spirit each day. She tirelessly attended to their son's needs, and her youth and lack of motherhood experience made every task overwhelming. She longed for guidance and support, but Richard offered none, leaving her to navigate the challenges on her own.

As Marva drifted further into the depths of depression, Richard's harassment intensified. His arrival home each day became a dreaded event, filled with verbal and emotional abuse that left her feeling worthless and stripped of any remaining self-confidence.

In the midst of this turmoil, Marva discovered that she was pregnant. Fear washed over her as she wondered how she could bring another child into such a toxic environment. She was 16 years old when she got pregnant with her second child. The weight of her circumstances felt unbearable, and she questioned her ability to protect and care for both her son and a new baby.

Marva's isolation deepened as she faced the harsh reality of her situation. Her mother, who lived far away, seemed oblivious to Marva's daily torment. The absence of support and concern from her own family added to her feelings of abandonment and despair.

As the pregnancy progressed, Marva's anxiety grew. She worried about the impact of Richard's abuse on her unborn child. The fear of bringing another innocent life into such a hostile environment weighed heavily on her heart. She yearned for her mother's presence, hoping for a glimmer of hope and understanding.

But her mother remained detached, seemingly unaware of the turmoil Marva faced. The lack of compassion and intervention from those who should have protected her left Marva feeling even more alone and helpless. She longed for someone to recognize her pain and offer a helping hand, but it seemed like she was invisible to the world.

As Marva's depression deepened, Richard's harassment only escalated. The weight of his constant verbal and emotional abuse became unbearable.

One evening, Marva mustered the courage to approach Richard with trembling hands. She took a deep breath, trying to steady her nerves before speaking.

"Richard," she began, her voice barely above a whisper. "I need to talk to you. It's important."

Richard glanced up from his work, annoyance written across his face. "What now?" he snapped. "Can't you see I'm busy?"

Marva's heart sank, but she pressed on, determined to share the news that had been weighing heavily on her. "I... I just found out that I'm pregnant," she confessed, her voice quivering.

Richard's face contorted with a mix of surprise and annoyance. "Pregnant?" he scoffed. "Are you serious? How did you let this happen?"

Marva's eyes filled with tears as she struggled to find the right words. "I... I don't know," she stammered. "I'm scared, Richard. I need your support."

Tension hung heavy in the air as Marva awaited Richard's response. But instead of offering reassurance or understanding, Richard's face turned cold, a sinister demeanor lurking behind his eyes.

"You know what?" he sneered. "That's not my problem. You're the one who can't keep things under control. Deal with it yourself."

Marva's heart sank even further, her fears amplified by Richard's callous response. But deep within her, a newfound determination began to burn.

Richard's anger simmered, his control slipping through his fingers. "You don't understand, Marva," he growled. "I've taken matters into my own hands. How about you abort the baby so that we won't have a problem with it anymore?"

Marva's eyes widened as she heard Richard's confession. Her determination burned stronger within her, fueling her next words.

"No, Richard," she declared, her voice steady and unwavering. "I will not let you control my body or our child's fate. My decision is to keep this baby, no matter what."

Richard's face twisted with anger, his control slipping further away. "You can't defy me, Marva," he seethed. "I won't allow it. This is for the best."

But Marva stood tall, a newfound strength radiating from her. "No, Richard," she said firmly. "I will protect my child, and I will protect myself. We deserve happiness, away from your toxicity."

Richard, enraged by Marva's defiance, reached out and grabbed her arm, his grip tight and bruising.

"You have no idea what you're getting yourself into!" he spat. "You'll regret this!"

But Marva, fueled by her determination and newfound strength, managed to break free from his grip. Her voice rang out, steady and resolute.

"I won't," she declared. "I won't let your abuse and manipulation continue any longer."

Without another word, Marva walked away, leaving Richard seething in his own anger and powerlessness. Marva's journey towards creating a better life for herself and her unborn child had begun, and she would not let anyone, including Richard, stand in her way.

Marva's mind raced, searching for a way out of the darkness that enveloped her. She longed for a safe haven where she and her children could find peace and rebuild their lives. But the path to freedom seemed elusive, and despair threatened to consume her.

To make matters worse, Marva found herself thrust into the daunting role of a caretaker for their son despite her young age and lack of experience. She was thrown into the deep end of motherhood without any knowledge or guidance, overwhelmed by the weight of her responsibilities. The combination of Richard's relentless harassment and her own insecurities pushed her further into the depths of a deep depression, a darkness that seemed impossible to escape.

But fate had a cruel twist in store for Marva. Just when she thought her life couldn't get any more challenging. The news brought forth a whirlwind of emotions - joy at the prospect of new life, fear, and uncertainty. However, Richard showed no interest in her well-being or the growing lives within her, adding to her already overwhelming burden.

Days turned into weeks, weeks turned into months, and months turned into years as Marva endured Richard's abuse and neglect. The weight of her loneliness and isolation became unbearable as she longed for solace and support. She yearned for someone to understand her pain and offer a helping hand, but her own mother was nowhere to be found. The absence of familial support only added to the heaviness in her heart, leaving her feeling utterly alone in her struggle.

But amidst the darkness, a flicker of hope began to emerge within Marva's heart. Sitting alone in her dimly lit kitchen, she realized she couldn't continue living like this, allowing Richard to control and manipulate her every move. With a newfound determination, she made a life-altering decision - she would escape this toxic relationship and create a better life for herself and her children.

Chapter 8:
A Grip on Hope

Marva's world had become a minefield of torment and despair. The weight of Richard's abuse bore down on her, a suffocating presence that seemed to grow heavier with each passing day. Despite the arrival of their new baby, the toxic cycle of harassment and physical and emotional abuse continued unabated.

The nights had become a haunting symphony of fear and dread. As Marva cradled her second baby, she felt the weight of her helplessness pressing down on her. The relentless harassment and unwanted advances from Richard had left her feeling vulnerable and exposed, a prisoner in her own home.

The news of her second pregnancy had sent shockwaves through Marva's already burdened heart. The fear of bringing another innocent life into the toxic environment she was trapped in gnawed at her soul. Each day, she grappled with the weight of her responsibilities, the suffocating grip of Richard's abuse, and the uncertainty of what the future held for her and her children.

The weight of her circumstances had become unbearable, and Marva found herself at a breaking point. The relentless abuse had chipped away at her spirit, leaving her feeling like a mere shadow of the vibrant young woman she once was. But within the depths of her despair, a flicker of defiance began to kindle within her.

A steely resolve welled up inside Marva as she thought of her pregnancy. She knew that she couldn't subject her children to a life tainted by Richard's toxicity. The safety and well-being of her children became her unwavering purpose, igniting a fierce determination within her to break free from the chains that bound her to Richard's abuse.

As Marva's pregnancy progressed, unfortunately, her second child with Richard didn't make it. On the day of delivery, the baby didn't cry. The doctors tried their best to revive their baby, but it was not enough. Marva cried a lot, and she never expected this to happen. She hugged her baby and said, " I'm sorry, baby. I'm sorry.

It was one of the saddest days in Marva's life when she came home. She was very angry at Richard because he acted like nothing happened; he was very happy and continued drinking.

With each passing day, Marva's resolve solidified, propelling her towards a path of liberation and self-preservation. She knew she had to find the strength to defy Richard's control and create a better life for her family, no matter the challenges ahead.

One evening, as Richard's menacing presence loomed over her, Marva found herself at a crossroads. The weight of her circumstances may have felt insurmountable, but a fierce strength had been awakened within Marva. With her children nestled in her arms, she mustered the courage to confront Richard, her voice steady and resolute.

"Richard," she spoke, her voice quivering but resolute. "I cannot endure this torment any longer. The weight of your abuse crushes me, but I refuse to let it consume us. I will not allow my children to grow up in this toxic environment."

Richard's face contorted with fury, his control slipping through his fingers."You have no idea what you're talking about, Marva," he spat, his voice laced with venom. "You're trapped here, and you'll do as I say."

Marva's gaze remained unwavering; her determination unyielding. "No, Richard," she countered, her voice steady and strong. "I will protect my children, and I will protect myself. We deserve happiness, away from your toxicity."

Enraged by Marva's defiance, Richard reached for her with menacing intent. His grip tightened around her arm, his fingers digging into her skin. "You have no idea what you're getting yourself into!" he hissed, his eyes burning with rage. "You'll regret this! No one defies me here."

Because of his drunkenness, He grabbed a machete and slapped Marva on her knee. She fell to the ground, begging for Richard to stop. "No! Richard, please stop. I'm begging you. Stop! I'm hurt.".

Richard's grip loosened slightly, a twisted satisfaction gleaming in his eyes. "That's what I said," he sneered. "You'll regret this! No one defies me."

Marva, her body trembling with pain and fear, managed to crawl away from Richard's clutches. Blood poured from her wounded knee as she struggled to escape. But in her darkest moment, a glimmer of hope emerged.

Her neighbor Lily, alerted by the commotion, rushed to Marva's side. "Marva, what happened to you?" she cried, concern etched across her face.

"Please help me!" Marva pleaded; her voice choked with tears. "I will go to the police station."

But Lily, wise in the ways of the world, shook her head. "No! You can't, not in this situation," she urged. "Let's go inside my house, and I'll treat your wound first."

Marva's heart ached as she saw her legs covered in blood, but she knew she had to stay strong. She promised herself that once she had recovered, she would seek justice for herself and her children. Despite the immense pain and fear, Marva knew that reporting the incident was the right thing to do.

Lily attended to her wound with gentle care, Marva's mind raced. The pain in her knee was excruciating, but her determination to bring her attacker to justice fueled her resolve. She couldn't let this act of violence go unpunished. With tears streaming down her face, she thanked her neighbor for her kindness and assured her that she would rest before taking any further action.

As Marva rested, Lily saw Richard in the yard, staring out the window. Richard knew that she was at Lily's house.

Lily, sensing Marva's unease, offered her support. "Do you want me to come with you to the police station?" she asked, her voice filled with compassion.

Marva shook her head, her voice filled with determination. "No, Lily. I'm fine," she replied. "I don't know what to do. I'm worried for my babies."

Lily's heart ached for the young woman before her. "You poor little girl," she whispered, her voice laden with sympathy. "At such a young age, you're experiencing these tragedies."

Marva's gratitude overflowed as she looked at Lily. "Thank you so much for what you've done, Lily," she said, her voice filled with emotion. "I need to go home; my babies are looking for me."

With a renewed sense of purpose, Marva stealthily made her way back to their house, using the back door to avoid Richard's notice. She saw him drinking, lost in his own world. Marva crept silently, her heart pounding in her chest, until she reached their room. With a mixture of relief and joy, she embraced her children tightly.

Days turned into weeks, and Marva's physical wounds slowly healed with time. The emotional scars, however, remained, as did her determination to seek justice. But she doesn't have the guts to do it;

she doesn't know how to file a report. At her young age, all she can do is cry and cry and wait until she is old enough to know everything.

Marva and Lily's friendship continued to blossom, bringing them closer together each passing day. The backyard had become their sacred space, a sanctuary where they could confide in each other without fear or judgment. The weight of their respective burdens seemed a little lighter in the presence of a kindred spirit.

Marva found solace in sharing her life stories with Lily, opening up about the abuse she had endured at the hands of Richard. Lily listened intently, her eyes filled with empathy and understanding. She offered words of comfort and encouragement, assuring Marva that she was not alone in her struggle. As Lily shared her stories of overcoming adversity, Marva felt renewed strength and hope.

One sunny afternoon, as they sat on the grass, Lily turned to Marva with a mischievous smile. "Marva, I have a little surprise for you," she exclaimed. "How would you like to go to the movies with me?"

Marva's eyes widened with excitement. Going to the cinema had always been her dream, but she wasn't sure if Richard would allow it. Lily sensed her uncertainty and reassured her, "Marva! Give yourself some free time; I don't think two hours is too much. You deserve to have a break."

Feeling a surge of courage, Marva made up her mind. "Yeah, I think that would be great for me to release the tension that I have right now. I will ask Richard."

Later that evening, Richard arrived home from work. Marva nervously watched as he started drinking alcohol, knowing that his mood could shift at any moment. Gathering her courage, she approached him. "Richard, can I go out for a little while? Lily invited me to watch a movie. It will be quick, and then I'll come home straight away."

Richard glanced at Marva, suspicion in his eyes. "Where are you going?" he questioned, his voice laced with anger.

Marva stammered, her heart pounding in her chest. "To the movies… with Lily. I promise I won't be late."

Richard contemplated for a moment, his eyes scanning Marva as if searching for deceit. Finally, he let out a sigh and reluctantly handed their baby over to Marva. "Fine. Go. Forget about cooking dinner," he muttered, his tone filled with resentment.

Marva's shock quickly gave way to tremendous excitement. She had been granted permission to go out, to experience something new and liberating. Gratefully, she rushed to change her clothes and meet Lily.

Arriving at Lily's house, Marva found her waiting eagerly at the door. "Marva, I'm so glad you're here! Let's go," Lily exclaimed, and the two friends embarked on their long-awaited adventure to the cinema.

For two blissful hours, Marva lost herself in the magic of the silver screen. She laughed, cried, and experienced a range of emotions she had forgotten were possible. It was the greatest day of her life, a taste of freedom she had never known before.

As they made their way home, Marva reached into her bag to search for her keys. Panic washed over her face as she realized they were missing. Frantically, she knocked on the door, calling for Richard to let her in. But there was no response, only silence.

Exhausted from her efforts, Marva collapsed onto the porch; disappointment etched across her features. Lily witnessed her friend's distress and called out to her. "Marva, why are you sitting on the porch? Is something wrong?"

Marva sighed; her voice filled with uncertainty. "I think Richard's not home, but the lights are still on. I don't know what to do."

Concerned, Lily insisted, "Come over, Marva. I'll prepare a room for you. I don't think anyone's there, and I don't want you to be alone."

Reluctantly, Marva followed Lily inside. She felt guilty for intruding, but she couldn't deny the comfort she found in her friend's presence. "Thank you, Lily," she said softly, "but I'll go back home first thing in the morning."

The night passed in a restless haze for Marva. She found herself unable to sleep, instead sitting by the window, her eyes fixed on the door, waiting for Richard to return. Anxiety consumed her, fueled by the worry for her children's well-being.

In the midst of her thoughts, Lily's voice broke through the silence. "Marva, I have something I need to tell you, "She said hesitantly. "I hope you won't be mad at me, but I saw a lady visiting your house late at night."

Confusion colored Marva's expression. "A lady? I don't know who that could be. I didn't notice anyone visiting us."

Lily's voice slightly trembled as she continued, "Marva, please don't be upset, but I think Richard may be seeing another woman. I saw them once, kissing. Marva was shocked to hear the news; she was stunned after knowing that Richard was bringing another woman while she was there. She got scared thinking about what would happen to their kids. "I don't care, Lily. I want to get out of that prison-like house, and I want to bring my babies out from him. That is all I care," Marva said.

Marva can't sleep; she's always staring out the window, waiting for Richard to open the door. She is really worried about her babies.

Chapter 9: Shattered Dreams

Months passed, and Marva's life got harder. Every day felt the same, filled with hurt and sadness. Richard's hold on her got stronger, and she couldn't find a way out.

Marva had to take care of her children and deal with Richard's mean behavior. She had so much to do around the house, which never seemed to end. It made her tired and sad.

Richard was being even meaner to Marva. He enjoyed seeing her hurt and used his power to show he was in charge. Every night, Marva had to deal with temperamental behavior towards her. It made her feel like she was just a part of his game.

Marva couldn't take Richard's cruelty anymore. She felt so sad and empty like all the happiness inside her had disappeared. Sometimes, she dreamed of escaping this terrible situation, but she was scared of what Richard might do if she tried to leave. The fear of him hurting her or their children was always there, making it hard for her to even think about leaving.

Then, something awful happened. Marva found out she was going to have another baby with Richard. It was like all the hope she had left was broken into tiny pieces.

The thought of having another baby with Richard scared her so much. She didn't know if she could protect this new baby from the bad things Richard did. It made her feel even more trapped and alone.

Marva felt a mix of feelings as her pregnancy progressed. She loved the baby growing inside her but was also scared of what life would be like for the baby with Richard around.

Marva's sister, Eve, unexpectedly came to visit her. Marva was shocked by Eve's arrival because she hadn't anticipated a family member reaching out to her. Tears welled up in Marva's eyes as she asked, "Eve, how are you? What are you doing here?"

Eve responded calmly, "Hey Marva, I'm fine. I came here to check on you. It's been a while since we last spoke. How's life been as a mistress?"

Marva pleaded, her voice filled with desperation, "Eve, please help me. I can't take it here anymore. Richard keeps abusing me. Get me out of here."

Eve's face contorted with a mix of anger and disappointment. She retorted, "This is all your fault. If you hadn't stolen our mother's boyfriend, you could've still been with us. Our grandmother won't accept you anymore. Where is Richard?"

Marva, though mad at Eve's accusation, expected this response. She chose not to engage and continued doing her chores as if she hadn't heard Eve's hurtful words. They still believe that I stole Richard from our mom, Sarah.

Eve's visit was not for me, but she just wanted to stay for the night since the road to the highway was very far and dark, so she decided to look for me. She then left first thing in the morning; she didn't even say goodbye to her sister. Marva found out that she was already gone.

Days turned into weeks, and Marva couldn't bear the torment any longer. The abuse had escalated to a point where it was no longer just verbal but also physical. Every day, she would put on a facade, doing her best to pretend everything was fine, but deep inside, the pain and fear were eating her alive.

She couldn't ignore her tiny spark of love for her unborn child.

Desperate for guidance and support, Marva confided in Lily, pouring out her pain and anguish. Lily also felt a deep concern for her friend, and together, they sought solace in their shared struggles.

Lily, determined to help Marva, couldn't bear to see her friend suffer any longer. She knew that Marva's life, and the life of her unborn child, hung in the balance. With a heavy heart, Lily confided in a close friend who worked at a local women's shelter, pouring out the details of Marva's dire situation and pleading for help. Her friend, a compassionate soul, promised to do everything within her power to assist Marva, providing her with a safe haven away from Richard's reach.

Marva, overwhelmed by fear and desperation, found solace in Lily's comforting presence. Tears streamed down her face as she spoke, her voice filled with anguish.

"Lily, I just don't know what to do anymore," Marva sobbed, her voice trembling with raw emotion. "I love my baby so much, but I'm terrified of what Richard will do to us."

Lily, ever by Marva's side, reached out and gently held her friend's hand. Her touch offered a small measure of comfort, a reminder that she was not alone in this fight.

"I understand your fear, Marva," Lily said, her voice filled with empathy. "No one should have to live in constant fear. We will find a way to protect you and your baby. You are not alone in this."

Marva sniffled, wiping away her tears with a trembling hand. The weight of her circumstances threatened to crush her, but Lily's unwavering support gave her a glimmer of hope.

"Thank you, Lily," Marva managed to utter, her voice choked with gratitude. "I'm grateful to have you by my side. I don't know how I would have managed without you."

Lily, her heart aching for her friend, squeezed Marva's hand gently. "You don't have to thank me, Marva," she assured her, her voice filled with sincerity. "We are friends, and friends look out for each other."

Marva's days were a blur of exhaustion and despair. The arrival of baby Ron brought a mix of joy and overwhelming responsibility. At just 19, she found herself caring for three young children, with Richard's oppressive presence casting a dark shadow over her every moment.

Despite the overwhelming challenges and constant cruelty, Marva tried her best to create a loving and nurturing environment for her children. Her heart swelled with love as she watched her children play together, but the weight of her circumstances ground that joy into grief. Richard, as always, demanded that she do everything in the house without lifting a finger to help care for the children. Her days were filled with constant responsibilities, from cooking meals, washing Richard's dirty clothes, and all of the household chores to bathing and clothing her children, all while trying to ignore the pain and exhaustion that plagued her every moment.

Marva's mental health deteriorated further due to the lack of support and understanding from Richard. The postpartum depression she experienced intensified her feelings of despair and hopelessness. She longed for a moment of rest and a glimmer of happiness, but it seemed like an unattainable dream.

Richard's control extended even to the family's finances. He withheld money from Marva, fearing that providing her with more resources might fuel her escape. His paranoia drove him to tighten his grip, leaving Marva and the children in a constant state of need and insecurity. He prevented Marva from talking to anybody, as she would gain confidence and determination in leaving him.

One day, the weight of Marva's circumstances pressed down upon her, threatening to crush her spirit. With Richard absent from home, she focused all her energy on caring for her children, a task that seemed to drain her of every ounce of strength. It was in this moment of exhaustion that she received an unexpected visit from Lily, her steadfast friend, who had brought along a companion named Lucy. Marva welcomed them into her backyard, seeking solace in their presence and the shared empathy that bound them together.

"I don't know how much longer I can go on like this, Lily," Marva confessed, her voice heavy with weariness. "It's just so exhausting."

Lily, her eyes filled with compassion, reached out and grasped Marva's hand in a show of solidarity. "I completely understand, Marva," she replied softly. "But remember, you're not alone in this. There are people out there who want to help."

Lucy, a survivor of her own abusive past, listened intently as Marva poured out her heart, her voice trembling with the weight of her pain. Tears welled up in Lucy's eyes as she witnessed the depth of Marva's suffering. Her heart ached for Marva and her children, and she resolved to offer her unwavering support.

"Marva," Lucy spoke gently, her voice filled with empathy. "I want you to know that I'm here to support you through this difficult time. I understand your situation, but why are you still staying?"

Marva hesitated; her mind filled with the haunting fear of what Richard might do if he found out about her intentions to leave. The thought of uprooting her life and the lives of her children seemed almost insurmountable. But as she looked into the eyes of Lily and Lucy, their determination and compassion shining through, a spark of hope ignited within her.

"How am I supposed to leave, Lucy?" Marva's voice wavered, and her fear showed. "I'm scared he'll come after me and the children. I don't have anyone else to turn to. My mother brought me here and left me with this man."

Lucy, understanding the depth of Marva's fear, spoke with gentle reassurance. "I understand your fear, Marva," she said, her voice filled with conviction. "But your safety and the safety of your children are our priority. We'll discreetly help you gather important documents and necessities, creating a plan that ensures your escape is as smooth as possible."

Together, the three women hatched a plan to ensure Marva's safety and provide a way out of this abusive relationship. Lucy shared information about local resources, including shelters that could offer Marva and her children a safe place to stay. She also emphasized the availability of counseling and legal support to help Marva break free from Richard's control.

"Thank you, Lucy and Lily," Marva whispered, her voice filled with gratitude. "I never thought I'd have people on my side like this. Your support means more to me than words can express."

As time slipped away, Marva suddenly realized the danger of being discovered. Richard would soon return home, and she couldn't risk him hearing their conversation or seeing their united front. She mustered the strength to speak up, her voice tinged with urgency.

"Girls, I really appreciate your advice, but I need you to go now," Marva pleaded, her eyes darting towards the approaching time. "Richard is coming soon. I don't want him to see or hear us talking about this."

Lily and Lucy understood the gravity of the situation, their own fear mirroring Marva's. They quickly rose from their seats, exchanging worried glances. They knew the risks, but their commitment to Marva's safety outweighed their own anxieties.

"If you need help, we are always here," Lily assured Marva, her voice filled with determination. "Take care of yourself and your children. We will continue to support you."

Secretly, Richard had been listening to their conversation from behind the bushes. His anger grew with every word he heard. The thought of losing control over Marva and their children fueled his rage, and he was determined to ensure they would never escape his clutches.

As Marva bid goodbye to Lily and Lucy, Richard watched their every move, carefully planning his next move. He knew he had to maintain his image of innocence and love towards Marva, ensuring she would never suspect his true intentions. Richard played the part perfectly, acting surprised when Marva turned to see him standing there.

"Hey, Marva, who were those women? What were you talking about?" Richard asked innocently, his eyes fixated on Marva's every move.

Startled and nervous, Marva stumbled as she tried to come up with an explanation. Her mind raced, trying to find a way to protect herself and her children. She decided to downplay the conversation, not wanting to escalate the situation further.

"Oh, Richard, it's just Lily, our neighbor, and her friend," Marva said, trying to keep her voice steady. "Nothing important, I promise."

Richard's gaze intensified, suspicion lingering in his eyes. He knew Marva was hiding something from him, and the thought enraged him even more. He took a step towards her, his tone changing from fake concern to veiled threats.

"Marva, this is the last time I will ask you. Tell me the truth," Richard growled, his voice laced with anger and control. "Who were they, and what were you talking about?"

Marva could feel her heart pounding in her chest. She knew she had to be careful with her words to protect herself and her children, yet she also understood the dangerous game she was playing.

"They were just offering some advice, Richard," Marva replied, praying her response would be enough to appease him. "Advice about being a better mother and handling our responsibilities. Nothing more, I swear."

"You better be telling the truth, Marva," Richard hissed. "Because if you're not, I will make sure you understand the consequences of going against me."

Richard left Marva and went inside. As Marva was struck and felt relief, she thought it was the end for her. She ran towards her children, and she hugged them. Tears are falling from her eyes, and she is dreaming of when this will be over.

A few days passed, and Marva carefully managed her moves, as she didn't want Richard to figure it out, but Marva didn't know that Richard had heard the conversation she had had with her friends.

A toxic mix of anger and fear fueled Richard's actions. He could feel his control slipping, and the thought of losing Marva and their children pushed him further into a dark and vengeful mindset as his trembling hand clutched the whiskey glass, the burning liquid searing down his throat as he drowned his thoughts in alcohol. The weight of their conversation hung heavy in the air, creating an oppressive atmosphere in their once peaceful home.

As Marva diligently did the dishes, her mind raced with fear and uncertainty. She had never seen Richard like this before, consumed by rage and drowning in a sea of doubts. She knew she had to stand her ground and defend herself against his accusations, even if it meant risking her own safety.

Suddenly, Richard lunged towards Marva, his grip tightening on her hair, his eyes blazing with a deadly mixture of anger and desperation. "You think you can just walk away from me?" he hissed, his voice dripping with venom. "I won't let you leave, not alive anyway. I bought you from your mother, you're now my possession."

Marva, her heart pounding in her chest, tried to remain as calm as possible. She knew any sign of fear or weakness would only fuel Richard's rage further. She mustered all her courage and looked him straight in the eye.

"Richard, please, I'm not planning to leave," Marva said, her voice steady but filled with a deep sadness. "I don't know if this is about my friends visiting me."

Richard's grip on her hair tightened, causing her immense pain. His face contorted with fury, and he unleashed a torrent of verbal abuse. "You think I'm stupid? I've heard enough. I know what you're planning behind my back."

Summoning every ounce of strength she possessed, Marva managed to wrench herself away from Richard's clutches. Gasping for air, she retreated, her back pressed firmly against the cool kitchen counter. Fear and defiance mingled within her eyes as she locked her gaze onto her violent and unstable partner.

"Don't you dare lay a finger on me again," she seethed, her voice quivering with a mixture of fear and determination. "I refuse to be a victim in this toxic relationship."

With every ounce of strength she could muster, Marva backed away from Richard, her eyes never leaving his malicious stare. "I'm leaving, Richard," she declared, her voice laced with defiance. "I will no longer be a prisoner of your anger and violence."

Richard's eyes widened in shock, his grasp on reality slipping away. He never expected Marva to challenge and defy him with such ferocity. As the weight of his actions crashed down upon him, regret mingled with his anger, creating a whirlwind of emotions within his tortured mind. "Do you think you have another place to go? Try me, Marva, try me," Richard said.

Marva raced to their room, afraid of what Richard would do next. She held onto the image of her children, their innocent faces, and the dream of a better future for them. As the night deepened and Richard was asleep, Marva seized the opportunity. She packed all of the things she needed, but she realized she couldn't take all of her three children together with their baggage, and she made the hardest decision a mother couldn't do: she left her youngest child, she hugged him so tight and said "don't worry I'll come back for you in no time" she promised.

Marva then slowly walked to the door carrying her two children, Mark and Marcia. Although the road ahead was daunting and uncertain, Marva knew she had made the right decision. She was no longer trapped in Richard's control. She said to herself, "I won't let you control me anymore, Richard, "her voice trembling but filled with determination. "I'm done living in fear."

They swiftly walked to her grandmother's house, where Marva and her children would find safety and solace. As they crossed the threshold of the house, Marva felt a weight lift off her shoulders, a glimmer of hope emerging from the darkness.

She knocked on the door, tears bursting out. "Hello, Grandma, open the door; it's me, Marva. Please help me." She was shocked when the person who opened the door was her mother.

Chapter 10: Escape from the Shadows

Marva was speechless when she saw her mother on the doorstep. Curiosity grew within her. "Why are you here?" Sarah asked. "I don't want to be there anymore," Marva heard herself say to her mother, bitterness in her tone. Richard, her mother's ex-boyfriend, had tormented her for far too long.

"Maybe he's just drunk or upset with something you did," Sarah's voice dripped with concern, attempting to defend Richard. But Marva knew better.

"Even if he's drunk or sober, I feel like I'm in hell! And where were you when I needed you?" Marva's voice shook with a mix of sorrow and anger, her tears flowing freely. She couldn't understand how her own mother had let her suffer at the hands of such a man.

"Do you want me to talk to him? It's just a misunderstanding," Sarah pleaded, her voice filled with desperation. But Marva had had enough.

"No! I don't want to go back there! It was your boyfriend! Why did you let me stay with him?" Marva's words exploded in the air, leaving a suffocating tension between mother and daughter.

Marva sank onto her bed, feeling a wave of exhaustion wash over her. She couldn't bear another moment in Richard's presence. Questions swirled through her mind, wondering if this was the beginning of their freedom or merely another chapter of misery.

Meanwhile, the next day, as Marva slept, Sarah stumbled upon Richard in the backyard. Her heart raced, fearing the conversation to come. Richard's eyes burned with anger as he confronted her.

"Sarah, do you know what your daughter did to me? Tell her to go home!" Richard's voice lashed out, venom dripping from every word. Sarah's heart sank, realizing the consequences of her choices.

"I'm so sorry, Richard. I will do my best to let Marva return as soon as possible. I promise you, this will be the last time," Sarah pleaded, her voice filled with desperation. She had to find a way to make things right, to protect her daughter from the monster she had unknowingly brought into their lives.

"You better do that, Sarah," Richard warned, his voice laced with a dangerous undertone.

As the anticipation built, Marva's fate hung in the balance. With her mother's resolve to rectify her mistake, the question remained - would she be able to escape the clutches of Richard's torment?

Marva, hey girl, wake up! It's morning now, get up and pack your things. It's time for you to go back home with Richard," Sarah said urgently. Drowsy and conflicted, Marva responded, "No, I already told you I don't want to go back. How many times do I need to tell you?" Frustration etched deep lines on Sarah's face as she retorted, "You hard-headed girl, why won't you listen to me? How will you feed and support your children, huh? Answer me!"

Determination filled Marva's voice as she looked Sarah in the eye, "I will find a job. I will do my very best to support my children." Sarah's frustration turned into anger as she lashed out, "How would you do that? You don't have an education. Are you even thinking straight, Marva?" Tears silently streamed down Marva's face as she realized the harsh reality of her situation.

With a heavy heart, Marva wiped her tears and slowly made her way back to Richard's house to retrieve her youngest child. Each step felt like a weight on her shoulders, and the thought of facing an uncertain future weighed heavily on her mind.

As Marva reached the house, she noticed that Richard was nowhere to be found. Panic gripped her heart as she searched frantically for her child. With trembling hands, she unlocked the door using the spare key hidden on the porch. The house was eerily silent, amplifying her fear.

Her worst fears materialized when she discovered her son was missing. Fear overwhelmed her, and tears flowed uncontrollably. Lily, her neighbor, spotted Marva's distress in her darkest moment and rushed to her side.

"Marva, I saw your child being taken by a woman yesterday. I think it might have been his sister because she called Richard brother," Lily said, offering a glimmer of hope. Relief flooded Marva's body as she clung to Lily for support.

Through her tears, Marva managed to express her gratitude, "Lily, I don't know how to repay you for all of this. Thank you so much." Lily enveloped Marva in a warm embrace and reassured her, "Don't worry, sister. I wish you nothing but the best in your new journey."

With newfound determination and the support of a kind neighbor, Marva felt a renewed strength within her. She knew her path would be challenging, but she was ready to face whatever came her way. As she embarked on this enticing new chapter of her life, Marva vowed to fight for her children's future and create a life filled with love and stability.

Marva's heart raced as she approached Richard's sister's house, her mind filled with a mix of determination and fear. She knew that reclaiming her youngest child would be a pivotal moment in her fight for freedom, but the uncertainty of the situation weighed heavily on her.

As she reached the doorstep, Marva's eyes fell upon her son, tears streaming down his cheeks as he sat alone and unseen in a crib. The sight pierced her heart, igniting a fierce determination within her. Without hesitation, she rushed to the door and took her son in her arms, his cries gradually subsiding as he felt the warmth and comfort of his mother's embrace.

"Martha, I'm here to get my child. Thank you," Marva said, her voice filled with a mix of gratitude and resolve. Richard's sister, taken aback by Marva's unexpected appearance, simply nodded, her expression a mix of shock and uncertainty.

With her son in her arms, Marva made her way back home, her heart heavy with the weight of the challenges that lay ahead. She knew this was just the beginning of a long and arduous journey, but the glimmer of hope in her son's eyes fueled her determination to fight for a better future.

As she held her son, Ron, close, a surge of emotions washed over her. Relief, fear and a fierce sense of protectiveness intertwined within her, propelling her forward on the path to reclaiming her freedom and ensuring the safety and well-being of her children.

When Marva arrived at her grandmother's house together with her youngest child, her mother began asking questions. "Marva, you have three kids. My God, how would you support them? How can you provide their food, their clothes, their studies?

Marva's heart sank as she faced her mother's skepticism. The weight of her responsibilities as a single mother of three children felt heavier than ever, and the doubt in her mother's eyes only added to her burden.

"I will find a job in order to support them. For now, I need your help in taking care of them, and I will also pay you, Mother," Marva replied, her voice filled with determination.

Sarah's frustration boiled over, and she lashed out at Marva. "Your optimism doesn't help you at all, stubborn kid," she added, her words cutting through the air like a sharp blade.

Despite her mother's disapproval, Marva remained resolute. She knew the road ahead would be challenging, but she was determined to provide a better future for her children, no matter the obstacles in her path.

Days turned into weeks, and weeks turned into months. Marva tirelessly searched for job opportunities, sending out countless resumes and attending interviews whenever she could. It was a challenging process, but she refused to give up. She knew she was one step closer to finding the right opportunity with every rejection.

Marva felt overwhelmed by the struggle to find a job without a degree or certificate. Each rejection made her feel worse, and her family's doubt made it even harder.

She started thinking about returning to school to have better opportunities for herself and her kids. But when she asked her family for help, they said no. Even her grandma, who let them stay with her, didn't support Marva's plan to study more.

Despite feeling discouraged, Marva's determination to create a better future for her family led her down a path of resilience and unwavering perseverance. Despite the challenges that came with working various jobs, from babysitting to washing dishes, she remained steadfast in her commitment to providing for her family's needs. She saved every bit she could for her studies, even though her income wasn't enough. She was determined to make things better, even without help from anyone, including Richard.

Every hard-earned penny became a stepping stone toward her ultimate goal. Each dollar set aside represented a beacon of hope, a testament to her unwavering determination to break free from the constraints of her circumstances.

With the limited savings she had managed to accumulate, Marva decided to enroll herself in a community school nearby. She believed it would be her chance to learn new skills, gain knowledge, and ultimately build a better life for her children. Marva knew that education was important for personal growth and crucial for becoming self-reliant and self-sufficient.

However, Marva soon realized that her financial situation made it difficult to afford the fees required for attending classes. Additionally, balancing work and studying proved to be incredibly challenging, as she couldn't afford to sacrifice her family's needs. Despite her initial determination, Marva made the difficult decision to drop out of school in order to prioritize her responsibilities as a provider for her family.

Marva knew deep down that her income would never be enough to provide for her children. Desperate and drowning in financial struggles, she found herself unable to pay her own mother back. One fateful day, Marva stumbled upon her mother sitting in the living room, surrounded by her three children. Gathering her courage, she approached her mother, pleading, "Mom, can I pay you next week? I'm short on funds right now." To her surprise, her mother replied with unexpected leniency, saying, "That's fine; just pay me whenever you have the money." The sudden change in her mother's attitude left Marva bewildered. Last month, her mother had been furious when Marva couldn't repay her. What on earth could have caused this sudden shift?

Unperceived by Marva, Richard, the father of her children, had been secretly supporting them all along. He had been providing money to Sarah, Marva's mother, without ever informing Marva. It was Sarah's twisted plan to allow Marva to struggle until she eventually returned to Richard. But Marva was determined to forge her own path, working tirelessly to earn and save money for her children's education.

However, everything changed when Marva realized she needed to pay for her youngest son's vaccination. Desperate and out of options, she made the reluctant decision to turn to Richard for help. Marva gathered herself and made her way to the gas station where Richard worked, approaching him with urgency. "Richard, we need to pay for Ron's vaccination. I don't have any money. Can you take care of this?" she asked desperately.

Richard, caught off guard, replied callously, "Wow, I thought you had it all figured out. Why do you still need my help?" Frustration boiled within Marva as she retorted, "This is not for me, Richard. This is for your son!" Eventually, Richard begrudgingly handed over the money. "This will be the last time I'll be giving you anything unless you decide to come back to me," he uttered with a hint of anger in his voice.

Unknown to Marva, Richard's anger grew within him, festering like a black cloud. He couldn't bear the thought of Marva moving on without him. In a fit of rage and a desire to teach her a harsh lesson, on a Friday night, Richard followed her secretly on her way home. With each step, his determination to confront her intensified.

The night was approaching, and there was no one around as Richard took the chance, his face concealed beneath a shirt, charged towards Marva. Startled, Marva turned around just in time to see Richard hurl a handful of dirt at her face. The particles stung her eyes, blinding her temporarily. In that moment of vulnerability, Richard seized the opportunity and lunged at her, his hands closing tightly around her neck.

Instinct kicked in, and Marva fought back with all her might. Drawing on her adrenaline, she managed to free herself from Richard's grip, using her height advantage to overpower him. Gasping for air, Marva looked into Richard's eyes, her voice filled with a mixture of fear and anger. "Even if I'm blinded or even if I just close my eyes, I know it's you, Richard."

But Richard, consumed by his twisted rage, then grabbed a wooden stick and brutally struck Marva across the head. Blood poured from the wound, staining her face, as she crumpled to the ground, her strength faltering.

Richard, overwhelmed with shock and regret, watched in horror as Marva lay bleeding before him. "Why are you stopping, huh?" she gasped, defying him even in her weakened state. "Finish the job and kill me because if you don't, I'll go straight to the police and report you!" Her words pierced the darkness, leaving Richard trembling with the weight of his actions. He reached out to help Marva up, his voice tremoring as he said, "I'm sorry, Marva. I don't know what came over me. There's a river nearby; let's go wash your wounds." Marva, not falling for his apparent remorse, responded with defiance. "Do you really think I would believe you? The damage has been done. Go ahead, do it. Kill me!"

"I won't let you go to the police, Marva; please let me clean that blood. There's a river downstream," Richard pleaded, blocking Marva's path toward the police station.

"No! Please leave me alone! I'll just go home," Marva replied, her voice trembling with fear.

Overwhelmed by the sheer terror of the consequences he would inevitably face, Richard desperately tried to ensure that Marva wouldn't escape and report the incident, so he followed her all the way to her grandma's house and stayed there for a while. He was standing outside the yard, keeping guard.

Chapter 11:
Fighting for Freedom

In the midst of chaos and despair, Marva's world crumbled as she felt the blood drain from her face. Dizziness clouded her mind, but her determination burned brighter than ever. Bound by the love for her children and the need for justice, Marva refused to let Richard go unpunished.

Ignoring pleas for rest, Marva pushed through the pain and made her way home. Her forehead still oozing blood; she could feel the weight of Richard's evil deeds pressing down on her. The image of her children suffering under his influence fueled her resolve, propelling her forward.

As soon as she arrived home from the incident, Marva's wounds were still fresh and seeping through her head. Anguish and anger coursed through her as she confronted her mother, who was oblivious to Marva's bloody appearance, diligently sewing.

"Mother?!" Marva's voice trembled, a mixture of anger and pain. "Uhm," Sarah nodded absentmindedly. Marva tried once again, her voice desperate, "Mother? Look at me! See what Richard did to me. You want me to go back to him?"

Marva's voice rang out in anguish, her suffering evident. Sarah, taken aback by the sight of her daughter, finally noticed her injuries. "What happened to you?" Sarah gasped, her concern finally surfacing.

"Richard tried to kill me," Marva replied, her voice filled with defiance. Sarah's response stung Marva deeply as she retorted, "Maybe you did something wrong to him?"

"No! I haven't done anything wrong. I will go to the police and report him," Marva declared with determination. The intensity of the situation hung heavy in the air as Marva resolved to seek justice for the brutal attack she had endured. "Don't do that; maybe there's some misunderstanding between you," Sarah replied, fearful of what would happen to Richard.

Eve (Marva's older sister) saw and heard her, and she then shouted. "Marva! Go to the police station and report that bastard. Let me come with you." Eve added. No! Don't interfere in this; that is their fight. Let her do whatever she wants." Sarah inserted.

Sarah noticed Richard standing outside, so she approached him. They began talking, and Richard handed over the groceries and Marva's purse that had been left behind during the incident. Marva caught sight of Richard and her mother, Sarah, conversing in the yard. She felt confused about why Richard was there, but she chose not to dwell on it. Marva's determination to seek justice didn't waver, even in her current state.

Suddenly, Sarah and Richard noticed Marva approaching them. "Marva, where are you going?" Sarah asked, concern evident in her voice. "I'm going to the police station," Marva replied firmly. "Hey, don't do it", Richard, unable to contain himself, interjected, Marva. Go to your uncle instead. He can wash and treat your wounds. Just don't go to the station." Sarah added.

Marva, resolute in her decision, responded to her mother, "The only people who can touch me are police officers, nurses, or doctors." She understood the importance of seeking professional help in her situation.

My Mother's Betrayal

Richard added his plea, hoping to convince Marva otherwise. "Please, Marva, I'm begging you. I'm sorry. If I can't change your mind, just let the police officers know that you were attacked by a burglar or a thief."

Marva couldn't believe what Richard had said. She stared at him with anger, rendered speechless by his words. Without responding, she turned and left both of them, her mind filled with a mix of emotions and thoughts about how to handle the situation.

As Marva made her way to the main road, she realized that she didn't have any money with her. The police station was quite far from her current location, so she thought of visiting her uncle Chris, who was her mother Sarah's older brother. When she arrived at her uncle's house, she discovered that he was not there. However, fortunately, her aunt was present.

Desperate for help, Marva approached her aunt and pleaded, "Auntie, please help me. I need to go to the police station." Her aunt was shocked when she saw Marva, still bleeding from her wounds. "Oh my God! What happened to you, Marva? Does your mother know about this?" Her aunt asked with concern.

"It's a long story, and I can't tell you everything right now," Marva replied, feeling pressed for time. "I need to rush to the station. Can I borrow some money for my fare?"

Her aunt, still in shock, handed Marva some money. "Here, take this. Can you wait for your uncle to arrive? We can accompany you to the station," she suggested.

Marva hesitated for a moment, grateful for her aunt's offer but aware of the urgency of her situation. "No, thank you, auntie. I don't have much time, but I appreciate your concern. I will go now."

With the money in hand, Marva hurriedly left her uncle's house, determined to reach the police station as quickly as possible.

She was struggling and nearly fainted, her head still throbbing from the brutal attack, she desperately sought help. Just as she reached the highway, a kind-hearted driver noticed her distress. Concerned, he rolled down his window and asked, "What happened to you, and where are you going? Let me give you a ride."

Grateful for the unexpected assistance, Marva explained her situation to the compassionate driver. She shared the horrifying details of her encounter with Richard, emphasizing the urgency of getting to the police station to report the incident. The driver listened attentively; his empathy evident in his eyes.

Without hesitation, the driver opened the passenger door and gestured for Marva to get in. As she settled into the seat, a sense of relief washed over her. She felt a glimmer of hope, knowing that she was no longer alone in this ordeal.

During the drive to the police station, the driver offered words of comfort, assuring Marva that she had done the right thing by seeking help and reporting the attack. His supportive presence provided a much-needed reassurance that not everyone in the world was like Richard.

Upon arriving at the police station, the driver accompanied Marva inside, ensuring that she felt safe and supported until she could speak with the authorities. He provided his contact information, expressing his willingness to testify if needed and offering any additional assistance that Marva might require.

As Marva walked through the doors of the police station, her heart pounded in her chest. The walls seemed to close in around her, but her determination held strong. She knew that sending Richard behind bars was the only way to ensure her children's safety and break free from the nightmare that had consumed her life.

Every step she took was a battle against her weakened body, but Marva persevered. The police officers looked at her with disbelief, unable to comprehend the strength that fueled her fragile frame. With tears streaming down her face, she poured her heart out, recounting the horrors she had endured.

The room fell silent, the weight of her words hanging heavy in the air. "Young woman! What happened here?" the police asked. "Please help me; Richard attacked me!" Marva replied. "Let's get you to the hospital; we need to treat your wounds first," the police said. "No, officer, get him; he might go and run away," Marva said. "Don't! You look bad in your condition; go to the hospital first, get back here, and we will get your statement." The police respond.

Marva agreed with the police that she needed to have her wounds treated first, as they were still bleeding. She requested that they pick up her friend and neighbor, Grace, to accompany her to the hospital. The police officers went to find Grace, and when they arrived, Grace was filled with worry and started crying upon seeing Marva. "What happened, my dear?" Grace asked, concerned.

"I'll tell you along the way. Please accompany me to the hospital," Marva replied, her voice filled with a mix of pain and determination. The police officers and Grace accompanied Marva to the nearest hospital, where she received medical attention for her wounds. The doctor assessed Marva's open and fresh wound and advised her to come back in the morning. Due to her exhaustion and lack of sleep, the doctor determined that they couldn't suture the wound at that moment. Instead, they covered it with a bandage and provided Marva with some pain relievers to help manage the discomfort.

Marva and Grace stayed at the hospital for a while, ensuring that Marva was stable and comfortable. They discussed the incident and the events leading up to it, providing some comfort and support to Marva.

They returned to the police station to provide her statement. The police took her statement and advised her that they would call her the following week after conducting their investigation and preparing the procedure to capture Richard.

After successfully reporting Richard to the authorities, Grace brought Marva to her own home. Grace took care of Marva, ensuring that she was fed, bathed, and provided with clean clothes. The tense atmosphere at Marva's home, made Grace insist that she stay with her for the night. "Once you get treated properly, you can go home. But for now, just stay here. You're safe," Grace reassured her.

Marva felt an overwhelming sense of gratitude towards Grace for her kindness and support. "Thank you so much, Grace. I don't know how to repay you for all of this," Marva expressed, her voice filled with genuine appreciation.

Grace smiled warmly at Marva and assured her, "You don't have to repay me, Marva." The next morning, Marva and Grace returned to the hospital for Marva's operation. Thankfully, the procedure was successful, and Marva started to feel much better. After her discharge, Marva went back home.

As she arrived, Marva was taken aback to see her mother waiting for her. To her surprise and dismay, Richard was also present, sitting on the couch. Marva's emotions were in turmoil, and she exclaimed, "What is he doing here? I don't want to see him ever!" Her frustration and anger towards Richard were apparent.

Sarah, appeared shocked by her daughter's reaction. "What did you do? What?" Sarah demanded, desperately seeking answers from her daughter.

Marva took a deep breath and spoke with determination. "It's over. I've already provided my statement to the authorities, and he will be arrested on Monday," Marva explained, she revealed that she had finally taken a stand and provided the necessary information to ensure justice would be served. Feeling emotionally drained, Marva made her way to her bedroom

Both Richard and Sarah were shock and realization washed over them. Richard's initial reaction was one of defensiveness, urging Sarah to take action. "You better do something about this," he said firmly before abruptly leaving the house.

Sarah stood there, her face reflecting a mix of emotions. She understood the gravity of the situation and the need to address it.

On a Monday morning, Sarah visited the police station to check the status. She was shocked when she heard her daughter's statement. She approached the officer and said, "Officer, I am the mother of the girl who came here last week." Sarah continued, "Hello, Madam. Thankfully, you are here. We are preparing a warrant for the arrest of a man named Richard."

The police officer responded, "No, no, no, Officer. That's not why I'm here. There's a misunderstanding. I request that you cancel the arrest!" Sarah said confidently, "I am utterly confused, Madam. Your daughter arrived here with blood running down her head, and now you want to stop the arrest of the man who violated your daughter?" The police officer replied.

"No! Cancel it. She doesn't have the right to report that man. She was the reason why that happened to her." Sarah's anger surged as she responded, "No, Madam! We can't do that. I apologize." The police officer said, "I'm her mother. She doesn't know what she's doing. Cancel the damn arrest." Sarah, now filled with anger, shouted back.

"Alright! Since you won't listen, the only way to cancel the warrant is for your daughter to come back here and withdraw her statement." The police officer informed her. Sarah, cursing and furious, left the police station and began walking home.

Marva and her grandmother were outside, washing the dishes, when they heard Sarah's voice in the distance. The sound of cursing and shouting caught their attention, and Marva's grandmother asked, "Is that your mother yelling?"

Marva paused for a moment, trying to make sense of the situation. "Yeah, I think so," she replied, her voice tinged with concern. "I'm not sure what she's doing." Sarah confronted Marva right away. 'Marva!' Sarah shouted. 'You come with me to the police station right now!'"

"Why do we need to go there?" Marva questioned; her voice laced with confusion. "The police will come here once everything is prepared," she added. "No, I want you to stop the report right now," Sarah demanded abruptly. "Why do you want me to stop it?" Marva asked, her bewilderment growing. "Because if you won't, you can't stay here at the house. Now choose," Sarah responded firmly.

Marva was left speechless, tears streaming down her face. She couldn't comprehend why her own mother would put her in such a predicament. She felt trapped; refusing her mother's command meant she would be left with nowhere to go. Reluctantly, Marva made the regrettable decision to give in and agreed to her mother's request.

Together, they went to the police station. As they arrived, an officer approached Marva. "Hey, little girl, I'm so sorry for this," he apologized sympathetically. "Your mother is causing quite a scene here. If the warrant isn't canceled, I know you truly want that man behind bars, but for the peace of your family, just do what your mom told you."

Marva's heart ached as she filled out the form to cancel the report. Tears continued to flow, a mixture of disappointment, confusion, and sorrow. And as she put her signature on the dotted line, she couldn't help but wonder why her own mother would put her in such a difficult position.

As the weight of this betrayal settled over her, Marva's determination to seek justice transformed into a steely resolve. With a sense of foreboding and uncertainty gripping her heart, she knew the path to justice would be fraught with obstacles.

Marva's mind raced, desperately trying to make sense of her mother's betrayal. She couldn't fathom why Sarah would choose to protect Richard, the man who had inflicted so much pain upon her own daughter. Anger welled inside Marva, fueling her determination to expose the truth and ensure justice prevailed.

With a heavy heart, Marva decided it was time to confront her mother. She couldn't bear to believe that her own flesh and blood would turn against her at such a crucial moment. As she walked back home, the weight of the truth burdened her steps, but she knew she had to face this head-on.

Upon entering the house, Marva found Sarah sitting in the living room, nervously fidgeting with her hands. Their eyes met, and for a moment, neither spoke. The silence hung heavy, suffocating the room until Marva finally found her voice.

"How could you, mother?" Marva's voice quivered with a mix of pain and anger. "I trusted you, and you chose to protect him, to betray me."

Sarah's eyes filled with anger, her voice shaking as well. "Marva, you need to keep your mouth shut. Richard is the solution so that you can have a better life." Her words spilled out.

Marva's heart sank, a wave of empathy crashing into her anger. She had always known Richard held some power over her mother, but to witness it in this way was soul-crushing. The realization that her safety had been compromised for their family's well-being shattered Marva's trust.

"But, mother, I can't let him continue to manipulate us. Do you want me killed? Did you see what he has done to me?" Marva pleaded; her voice filled with desperation. Marva's mind was filled with questions as she thought about her mother's involvement with

Richard. With a mix of confusion and frustration, she repeated the questions, "Why, mother? Why? What hold does he have over you?"

Sarah nodded, "I don't know what you're talking about and I don't care, Marva. This will be a lesson for you if you do not go to him; you might experience the same situation again." So, pack your bags and bring your children, go home to Richard." Sarah said.

"How could you? You don't have the right to control me again, never!" Marva replied with tears streaming down her face.

Chapter 12: Rebuilding a Life

Marva's heart trembled with a mix of sadness and anger as she realized the depth of her mother's betrayal. At that moment, something inside her changed. She knew she had to break free from the toxic cycle that had entrapped her for far too long. She would no longer be a victim but a survivor. Marva was determined to create a different future for herself and her children, filled with love, resilience, and independence.

With her wounds still fresh and her body aching, she no longer wanted to subject herself and her children to a life of fear and abuse. Instead, she sought solace in the idea of education and empowerment. She realized that knowledge was the key to unlocking the doors of opportunity and breaking the chains that had bound her for so long.

With the savings she had managed to accumulate, Marva found an organization that provided training for practical nursing and first aid nearby and enrolled herself. This would be her chance to learn new skills, gain knowledge, and build a better life for her children. Marva wasn't simply pursuing education for the sake of personal growth; she also saw it as a way to become self-reliant and self-sufficient.

Marva was faced with a difficult decision, unsure if it was worth it. It weighed heavily on her as she questioned who would care for her children while she pursued her training. However, she also contemplated how she would be able to support her children in the long run. Despite her confusion, Marva knew that there was no turning back. She made up her mind to bring her children along and began packing their belongings, catching the attention of her mother, Sarah, who entered the room.

"Where are you going, Marva?" Sarah asked, concern evident in her voice. With a determined look, Marva replied, "I have been accepted into a prestigious institution that offers practical nursing training. I have decided to take my children with me to Ocho Rios and find a place for us to stay." Uncertain, Sarah questioned Marva's ability to manage the responsibility, asking who would look after her babies. Marva responded, busy with preparations, "Don't worry, I will find a way there."

Sarah worriedly contemplated the fate of her grandchildren, especially her attachment to Marva's eldest, Mark. Seeking advice, she turned to her own mother. "Mother, Marva is leaving. She plans to take the kids with her," Sarah revealed. Her mother inquired, "Why? And where are they going?" Sarah explained, "It's for her education."

"But who will take care of the children?" her mother asked. "Marva said she will find a way," Sarah replied. "I'm just worried about the kids, especially Mark. He's become like my own son." Sarah's mother sighed and looked concerned. "I understand that Marva wants to better herself, but she also needs to think about the well-being of her children. Have you talked to her about finding a support system or getting help?" she asked. "I've tried, but she seems determined to make it work on her own," Sarah replied. "I just hope she knows what she's doing."

With all their belongings packed and her children ready, Marva emerged from the room to find her grandmother and mother engrossed in conversation. "Grandma, Mother, we are about to leave. Thank you both so much for your help," Marva said, grateful. Her grandma halted her, asking, "Wait, Marva? Are you absolutely sure about what you're doing?" Overwhelmed with conviction, Marva replied, "Yes, I have already made up my mind. I have no other choice. I need to do this for the future of my family." It was then that her grandma made a surprising suggestion. "Just go by yourself, leave the children. We will take care of them. But your mother and I can't do it alone. I don't want you to forget your responsibility," her grandma pleaded. Her mother agreed with her grandmother, "I agree, Marva." Marva was stunned by her grandmother's unexpected offer, struggling to comprehend the situation. Overwhelmed with gratitude, she embraced her grandmother tightly and thanked her profusely, tears of joy streaming down her face. "Thank you, grandma. I promise I will never forget this.

As Marva walked through the doors of the establishment, her heart pounded with both trepidation and excitement. She knew this was the first step to reclaiming her life and building a better future. The walls of the institution seemed to radiate warmth and hope, washing away the memories of her past struggles. Marva was determined to make the most of this opportunity, no matter the challenges that lay ahead.

With each passing day, Marva's resilience and determination grew. She immersed herself in her studies, embracing the community school's knowledge and skills. She proved to be an exceptional student, driven by her past experiences and fueled by the desire to create a different life for herself and her children.

Though the road was challenging, Marva's determination and the unwavering support of friends and the shelter allowed her to rewrite her story. She transformed from a young woman trapped in despair to a warrior, fiercely protecting her children and defying the odds stacked against her.

Gone were the days of fear and oppression. Marva's story became one of resilience, strength, and hope. As she watched her children grow into confident, vibrant individuals, she knew she had made the right choice to seek help, believe in herself, and break free from the chains that had bound her for far too long.

Marva's journey began with her graduation from training, where she received a well-deserved certificate. Although her family couldn't be there to witness this proud moment, Marva's sense of accomplishment remained unshaken. She diligently applied for positions in various hospitals without wasting a moment, determined to fulfill her dream. She submitted her resume to countless companies, eagerly awaiting positive news.

Weeks flew by, but Marva was left disheartened as not a single response arrived. No letters or calls from the companies she had applied to. However, her unwavering determination persisted despite this setback. And so, the very next day, Marva made her way to the general hospital, full of hope as she walked in to submit her job application. It had always been her dream to be a part of the medical team, and she was brimming with confidence due to the training she had undergone. She knew she could do it.

Marva headed straight to the Human Resources Department, eager to make her case. As she waited there, anxiously anticipating her turn, suddenly, her name was called. With a mix of excitement and nervousness, she entered the room. The staff greeted her with a smile but also confusion, "Hi, we discovered that we received your application a year ago," the staff said. "Your name is a name that is not easily forgotten, when I saw your name, I remembered it. We also sent you a letter inviting you for an interview, but it appears that you were tagged as a no-show, Unfortunately, we cannot accept your application now, as many other candidates are vying for this opportunity. I'm truly sorry for the inconvenience," she added.

Confused and shocked, Marva quickly replied, "I'm sorry, but I never received any letter." Her frustration evident, she continued, "We must have sent it to the wrong address." The staff handed over the logbook, revealing the address they had used – Richard's address. Marva's anger boiled within her. How could Richard, even in his absence, continue to cause her misery?

With mixed emotions, Marva stormed out of the room, her head held high. She couldn't believe that Richard was still able to bring her such frustration, even though he was no longer a part of her life.

Despite the bad news, Marva's spirits immediately lifted when she received a letter offering her a job at an infirmary. She wasted no time and eagerly attended the interview.

Driven by her high hopes and determination, Marva aced the interview and secured the job. Excitement filled her heart as she embarked on this new chapter of her career. Marva's skills and expertise blossomed as time passed, reaching new heights. The infirmary recognized her relentless dedication, showering her with accomplishments and acknowledgments.

Marva was glad that she could fully support her family now, providing for their needs without facing any hardships; she even supported her grandmother and her mother at the same time. She felt grateful for the opportunity to be in a position to give back to her loved ones and create a comfortable life for them.

Marva believed that she had finally found her happily ever after within the walls of the infirmary. However, fate had a different plan in store for her. An unexpected incident threw her world into chaos, shaking the very core of her existence.

In the eerie confines of the infirmary, Marva found herself working the graveyard shift on the female ward. Little did she know that this night would forever be etched into her memory as one of the most horrifying encounters she had ever experienced.

One of the patients, Carmen, had a serious mental health problem. Sandra, who is Marva's coworker, oblivious to what was going to happen, went into Carmen's room to check her vital signs. But then, something terrible happened.

To her absolute disgust, Marva's colleague found a basin overflowing with human waste next to Carmen's bed. They needed to get rid of it, but Carmen refused to do it. She shook her head and said no.

Marva stood at the door, helping another patient, and tried to listen. She saw her coworker getting more and more frustrated, grabbing Carmen's hands and telling her to empty the basin. Carmen got mad and threw the waste from the basin, soaking herself and Sandra.

Sandra got really angry and noticed a curtain rod in the room. She took it and started hitting Carmen with it over and over again. Carmen was getting hurt with each strike. Marva couldn't do anything but watch in horror.

The brutal attack continued until Sandra pulled Carmen's right hand and dragged her, hurt and broken, out of the room towards the restroom. Marva couldn't stand by any longer and rushed inside as soon as her coworker left. She found Carmen struggling to put on her shirt, unable to use her right hand and shaking. Marva could see Carmen was upset, so she tried to help her, gently guiding her arm through the sleeve and bringing her back to her room.

Marva hesitated to report it because she was scared. Besides the fact that it was her senior, she didn't want to get into trouble that would affect her job and impact her family's support. So, she went to the restroom, locked herself in, and cried. She couldn't believe what had happened.

The very next day, their matron (head nurse) asked Marva to meet her at her office. The matron knew what had happened since Sandra had told her about it. However, she didn't want anyone else to find out.

It could tarnish their infirmary's reputation, which the government supported.

Marva felt a heavy pressure. She was concerned about Carmen's situation, wondering if it would happen again. Unable to sacrifice her job because of her family, Marva reluctantly agrees to keep it a secret solely for the sake of her work.

The resident doctor came to visit Carmen, accompanied by the matron. The doctor was puzzled when he noticed bruises on Carmen's body. As he gently touched her right arm, Carmen winced in pain. The matron explained that Carmen's behavior had changed and that she had been experiencing nightmares.

Suddenly, Carmen burst into tears and grabbed the doctor's hand, begging for help. "I need to tell you something," she pleaded. The matron swiftly pulled the doctor aside, insisting it was time for him to visit the next patient. Confused, the doctor insisted on hearing what Carmen wanted to say.

The next day, the doctor approached the matron privately, expressing his concerns and asking for more information about Carmen's condition. The matron seemed taken aback by his questions but reluctantly provided him with a file containing Carmen's medical history.

As the doctor analyzed the file, he realized that there was no clear pattern of recurrent abuse and neglect. It was evident that Carmen's injuries were not a result of accidents or nightmares but were the consequence of intentional harm inflicted upon her.

The doctor felt a mix of anger, guilt, and a strong desire to protect Carmen from further harm. He knew he had to take immediate action to ensure her safety.

Without hesitation, the doctor reported his findings to the hospital's administration, specifically mentioning the matron's attempts to hide the truth and suppress the incident. He also contacted the appropriate authorities to investigate the matter further.

An investigation was launched within days, and the nurse was immediately fired pending the outcome. Carmen was transferred to a different facility with a specialized team to address her physical and emotional needs.

As for Marva, she was relieved that the truth was finally brought to light, but she was also being questioned since she was also on the same shift. Marva was required to create a report on why she didn't speak up after witnessing this form of abuse or neglect.

Chapter 13:
From Darkness to Hope

Marva found herself in a difficult situation when she witnessed a troubling event unfold. She felt frightened and unable to express herself, which led to her decision not to report it. Marva did not want to get involved in the trouble at hand. Marva was invited by the parish council, who were the directors of the infirmary, to share her witness testimony on the incident. The council members stared at her, waiting for an explanation.

Feeling the weight of their expectations, Marva took a deep breath and began to recount the incident. She spoke honestly, detailing what had transpired despite her heart pounding with anxiety. The council members listened intently; their frustration evident on their faces.

"Why didn't you submit an incident report?" one of the members asked, their voice filled with disappointment.

Marva hesitated for a moment, unsure of how to respond. She knew deep down that covering up the incident was a mistake, but she was only trying to protect her colleague. She believed in second chances and didn't want to see her lose her job.

"I... I thought I could handle it on my own," Marva finally confessed. "I didn't want to cause any trouble for anyone."

The council members exchanged glances, realizing the complexity of the situation. While they appreciated Marva's loyalty, they also understood the importance of transparency and accountability.

"You should have informed us immediately," one of the council members said sternly. "We could have taken appropriate action and addressed the issue promptly."

Marva hung her head in shame, regretting her decision. She knew she had let down the council, the infirmary, and its patients. The consequences of her actions were now unavoidable.

"I'm sorry," Marva muttered quietly, her voice filled with remorse. "I didn't mean for things to turn out this way."

The council members sighed, their anger slightly dissipating as they realized Marva's genuine remorse. They recognized that her intentions had been rooted in her desire to protect her colleague, even if misguided.

Unfortunately, one of her colleagues, who also happened to be a neighbor, took it upon themselves to spread rumors about Marva stealing her mother's boyfriend. The humiliation and constant gossip deeply affected Marva, causing her to feel angry and frustrated. It also affected her superiors' and the director's decision to fire her. People discussed the situation openly, even in front of her, making it challenging for her to focus on her work.

Marva, however, remained determined to persevere despite the negative impact on her performance. She knew she had to support her entire family and could not sacrifice her job because of her colleagues' hurtful actions. Just when it seemed like things couldn't get any worse, a stroke of good fortune came her way. One of the matrons working in the infirmary also had a position at the prestigious general hospital. She had become close friends with Marva and took notice of her exceptional skills and unwavering resilience.

One day, the matron called Marva into her office for a conversation. "Marva, I can see how you've been ignoring the hurtful remarks, but I can't stand to see you suffer anymore," the matron said compassionately. "Thank you for your kind offer, Miss, but I've learned to handle bullying and use it as motivation," Marva responded gratefully. Not willing to let Marva suffer any longer, the matron handed her an application letter. "Take this letter, change the name to yours, and consider it an invitation to join the general hospital," the matron said excitedly.

Marva was utterly shocked by the gesture. "Oh my! Is this an application letter to the general hospital?" she exclaimed. The matron nodded eagerly and reassured her, "Yes, my dear. With your talent and dedication, you belong there." Marva's heart swelled with gratitude at the thought of leaving behind the toxic atmosphere and embracing a new opportunity. A week passed, and Marva and the matron made their way to the general hospital together. This was Marva's third application, and this time, everything felt different.

Marva was absolutely astounded by the extensive series of examinations she had to undergo during her interview process. However, her unwavering determination and the fact that this was her dream job kept her going. Miraculously, Marva passed her application at the hospital and felt an overwhelming sense of happiness and gratitude. Not only was this position fulfilling personally, but it also provided her with an additional source of income.

The following day, Marva gathered the courage to render her resignation at the infirmary. Despite the negative comments and gossip that her coworkers threw at her, she responded with grace and maturity. Marva even went as far as to wish them happy lives and successful careers. She expressed her heartfelt gratitude to her superiors and those who had assisted her along the way.

The very next day marked the beginning of Marva's career at the prestigious General Hospital. Initially, nerves threatened to overwhelm her, but her matron, who oversaw the training of new hires, offered unwavering support. She encouraged Marva to study and familiarize herself with various medicines and the medication process. Marva's eagerness to learn was palpable; even after working long shifts, she continued to dedicate her time to studying. As a result, Marva's performance stood out from the crowd. Within her very first week, she received an abundance of commendations from the doctors she worked with. Pride filled her heart, and she couldn't have been happier.

Years flew by, marked by Marva's unwavering dedication to her job. She succeeded in providing her children with quality education through her hard work. Each of her children had completed their studies and obtained their own degrees. Her son Mark became a skilled welder, her daughter Marcia pursued a rewarding career as a nurse practitioner, even choosing to live in Canada, and her youngest son Ron proudly served as a police officer.

However, Marva's love and care extended beyond her immediate family. She also devoted herself to looking after her sister Eve, including her three kids, her mother, and her grandmother, ensuring they received the utmost support and affection they deserved. In doing so, Marva demonstrated the compassion and kindness that had brought her so much success throughout her career.

Marva's incredible journey is a testimony to the power of determination and perseverance. She defied all odds and succeeded in achieving her dream job and providing her loved ones with a secure future. As the years turned into decades, Marva's legacy continued to inspire those around her, serving as a living reminder that hard work and dedication can lead to a truly fulfilling and rewarding life.

Chapter 14: Unexpected Ending

Marva had dedicated a number of years of her life to working tirelessly in the bustling corridors of the general hospital. She had always believed in the power of healing and cared deeply for her patients, finding solace in bringing comfort to those in need. But Marva's journey was not solely filled with happiness and joy but marked by moments of unparalleled grief.

In 2005, when the world seemed to make sense to Marva still, tragedy struck her family. Her grandmother was unexpectedly taken away by a devastating stroke. The loss was sudden, leaving Marva and her loved ones grappling with a void that seemed impossible to fill. Grief consumed her, intertwining with her dedication to her work at the hospital.

As Marva tried to find her footing again, fate dealt her yet another cruel blow. Just five months after her grandmother's demise, her mother, Sarah, also left this world without warning. Marva's heart shattered into a million pieces, for she had not gotten a chance to give her loved ones the abundant life they deserved. All the while, she had been striving tirelessly to repay them for the love and support they had selflessly provided.

With her family gone, Marva's world turned into a bleak landscape. Her siblings, burdened by their own grief, struggled to carry on. Marva's children, whom she had poured her love and energy into raising, were now scattered across different paths, unable to come together as they once had. Though Marva had always been proud of her children's independence, the absence of their presence only intensified her loneliness.

Years rolled on, and Marva tried to pick up the pieces of her life, continuing to dedicate herself to her work. The hospital became her sanctuary, her escape from the harsh realities of her new reality. She found solace and purpose as she tended to the sick and comforted the wounded, even as her heart ached.

Fast forward to 2017, one day, Marva received a phone call from her granddaughter Mary, the daughter of her first-born son Mark. Mary's voice was filled with anticipation as she spoke, "Grandma, I'll be in St. Ann this coming Saturday for a project, and I need to find a place to stay. With my budget right now, I can't afford a hotel for a week. Do you know someone I can talk to about this?"

Marva smiled warmly, knowing she had a solution. "You can call your Uncle Ron. He has the keys to the house where your grandfather Richard and I used to live. I don't think anyone's living there now, so you can stay there whenever you need."

Gratefully, Mary replied, "Thanks, Granny. I'll give Uncle Ron a call right away." She dialed the number, but Uncle Ron's busy tone greeted her. Determined to reach him, Mary left a voicemail, "Hi Uncle Ron, it's Mary, your niece. I need to ask for a favor. Grandma mentioned that I can stay at the house for a week. It's for a school project, and I'll be in St. Ann next week."

A short while later, Mary noticed that Uncle Ron had called her back. However, she was unable to answer the call and instead found a voicemail waiting for her. She pressed play, her excitement turning into confusion and disappointment as she listened to Ron's message.

"Mary, I don't think you can stay at the house and when does your grandma have the authority over the house? She was just a minor when she was with my father. She doesn't have any right to the property she couldn't sign any legal documents, because she was a minor at that time. All I know is that your great grandmother was the one who signed the contract. Tell your grandmother that you can't stay here, and that it's impossible. Goodbye."

Mary's heart sank as she absorbed Ron's words. She hurriedly sent the voicemail to her grandmother, along with a message, "Granny! Uncle Ron said I can't stay there. I didn't listen to the whole message, but I've sent it to you."

Marva's brows furrowed with anger and concern as she listened to the voicemail. She dialed Uncle Ron's number, hoping for an explanation, but he refused to pick up the call. Frustrated, Marva decided to take matters into her own hands. She immediately transferred money to Mary's account, accompanied by a text message, "My dear, book yourself a room in a hotel. I won't let this ruin your project. Take care, my love."

Marva couldn't bear the weight of her own child's unexpected and unacceptable behavior, and she felt a deep sense of disappointment. Seeking solace, she decided to return to the place where she and Richard had once shared a life together. However, as she approached the familiar house, she noticed a letter lying on the doorstep. Marva quickly picked it up and saw that it was addressed to her. With trembling hands, she tore open the envelope and read its contents. To her astonishment, the letter revealed that she owed taxes on the property and that immediate payment was required. Her eyes widened as she scanned the document, and she couldn't help but notice her own name listed as the sole owner.

She couldn't recall ever signing any legal documents during her time with Richard. Determined to uncover the truth, Marva knew she needed expert guidance. She made an appointment with a reputable lawyer to verify the legitimacy of the document. Anxiously, she walked into the lawyer's office, clutching the letter tightly and hoping for answers. The lawyer carefully examined the letter, comparing it to property records and conducting thorough research. After a meticulous review, the lawyer confirmed that her mother had signed the title, designating Marva as the sole owner of the property. She was indeed the legal owner of the property. Shock and confusion washed over her as she struggled to comprehend the situation. Leaving the lawyer's office, Marva felt a whirlwind of emotions. She couldn't fathom how this had come to be. Memories of her time with Richard flashed before her, and she wondered why he had made her the owner without her knowledge or consent. Determined to find clarity, she embarked on a journey to uncover the truth behind Richard's actions.

Shock coursed through Marva's veins as she struggled to comprehend why the document bore her name. Memories flooded back, and with each piece of the puzzle falling into place, Marva realized there was more to this than met the eye.

Connecting the dots, she became curious about why Richard had made her the joint tenant. It seemed impossible for him to have done this, considering the abuse he had inflicted on Marva. But as she recalled, it all became clearer when she remembered her mother's role in orchestrating her life with Richard. She couldn't believe she had signed the contract with her young conscience and innocence. It dawned on her that her mother had planned this all along, using her as a pawn to gain control of the property. Everything fell into place - her mother's unwavering protection of Richard, even when he was clearly in the wrong.

Marva collapsed to the ground, utterly devastated by this revelation. She hadn't expected any of this to transpire, and the sad reality was that she couldn't confront her mother about it anymore. She had passed away, leaving Marva to grapple with the truth alone.

Marva's mind spun with thoughts of how to clear her name and prove her innocence in stealing Richard from her mother. Was this yet another layer to the complex story of her life? Did her mother's secret plan extend beyond just her living arrangement? These questions overwhelmed Marva, leaving her feeling trapped and unsure how to proceed.

Desperate for answers and resolution, Marva knew she had to find a way to uncover the truth. She resolved to delve deeper into her past, seeking any clues or evidence that could shed light on the true nature of her relationship with Richard and her mother's involvement. It would be a challenging journey, but Marva was determined to uncover the hidden pieces of her history and clear her name once and for all.

Authors Biography

Step into the captivating life and inspiring journey of Sonia Brooks, a remarkable woman from the enchanting island of Jamaica, West Indies. Born with an unwavering spirit and an insatiable thirst for knowledge, Sonia's path to success has been nothing short of extraordinary.

Her educational journey began at the prestigious Chester All-Age School, where she discovered her passion for learning and nurturing others. Eager to expand her horizons, Sonia went on to attend the esteemed Marcus Garvey Secondary School, where she laid the foundation for her exceptional career.

Fueled by her unwavering commitment to making a difference in the lives of those in need, Sonia embarked on a transformative course in first aid and practical nursing. With unwavering determination, she obtained both certificates from the prestigious St. John Ambulance Association, paving the way for her remarkable future.

Embracing her calling, Sonia dedicated thirteen-plus years of her life to serving at the renowned Public General Hospital, where her compassionate care touched the lives of countless individuals. Her expertise and genuine desire to uplift others became synonymous with her name, earning her accolades and respect within the medical community.

Driven by a longing for new opportunities and greener pastures, Sonia's quest for growth took her to the picturesque Cayman Islands. However, destiny had other plans in store for her. With unparalleled resilience, she navigated the challenges that came her way, always striving for a better tomorrow.

Finally finding her footing in the mesmerizing Turks and Caicos Islands, Sonia obtained a coveted work permit, opening doors to a new chapter in her life. With a heart overflowing with empathy, she embraced her role as a caregiver, dedicating nearly six years to caring for a cherished patient. She provided solace and comfort during their most vulnerable moments through her unwavering commitment and unyielding support.

When faced with the loss of her patient, Sonia's indomitable spirit urged her to seek fresh possibilities. She set her sights on the land of opportunity, Canada. In November 2009, she embarked on a remarkable journey that would forever shape her future.

Eager to carve her path in this new land, Sonia's tenacity led her to overcome the initial employment hurdles, defying the odds and making destiny work in her favor. Serendipity smiled brightly upon her when she crossed paths with her soulmate, Glenton Brooks. In a beautiful union of hearts and dreams, they found solace in each other's embrace, embarking on a new chapter together.

Now a beloved resident of the vibrant city of Brampton, Ontario, Sonia's story is a testament to the immeasurable power of resilience, perseverance, and unwavering compassion. Her journey serves as a shining example of how one woman's unwavering determination and fearlessness can pave the way for a bold and prosperous future.

With a heart committed to making a difference and an unwavering spirit that knows no bounds, Sonia Brooks continues to inspire and uplift, leaving an indelible mark on the lives she touches. Her story is a testament to the boundless potential within each of us, urging us to embrace our dreams and forge our own unique paths.

www.ingramcontent.com/pod-product-compliance
Ingram Content Group UK Ltd.
Pitfield, Milton Keynes, MK11 3LW, UK
UKHW061222180426
11947UKWH00026B/1961